ROMAN POLITICAL LIFE
90 B.C.–A.D. 69

Edited by T.P. Wiseman

EXETER STUDIES IN HISTORY No. 7
Published by the University of Exeter 1985

First published 1985 by the University of Exeter
Reprinted 1986

EXETER STUDIES IN HISTORY

General Editor: Colin Jones

Editorial Committee

Mrs B.J. Coles, BA MPhil FSA
M.D.D. Newitt, BA PhD FRHistS
M. Duffy, MA DPhil
Professor I.A. Roots, MA FSa FRHistS

Publications

No 1 *The Military Revolution and the State 1500–1800*
        edited by Michael Duffy
No 2 *Government, Party and People in Nazi Germany*
        edited by Jeremy Noakes
No 3 *'Into Another Mould': Aspects of the Interregnum*
        edited by Ivan Roots
No 4 *Problems and Case Studies in Archaeological Dating*
        edited by Bryony Orme
No 5 *Britain and Revolutionary France: Conflict, Subversion and Propaganda*
        edited by Colin Jones
No 6 *Nazism 1919–1945 A Documentary Reader 1:*
        The Rise to Power 1919–1934
        edited by J. Noakes and G. Pridham
No 7 *Roman Political Life 90 BC–AD69*
        edited by T.P. Wiseman
No 8 *Nazism 1919–1945 A Documentary Reader 2:*
        State, Economy and Society 1933–39
        edited by J. Noakes and G. Pridham
No 9 *Africa, America and Central Asia:*
        Formal and Informal Empire in the Nineteenth Century
        edited by Peter Morris
No 10 *'Raleigh in Exeter':*
        Privateering and Colonisation in the Reign of Elizabeth I
        edited by Joyce Youings
No 11 *The First Portuguese Colonial Empire*
        edited by Malyn Newitt

Exeter University Publications,
Hailey Wing,
Reed Hall,
Streatham Drive,
Exeter EX4 4QR

ISBN 0 85989 225 5
ISSN 0260 8628

Printed and Bound by A. Wheaton & Co. Ltd., Exeter

307370

Contents

Acknowledgements   Page iv

Chronological Table   Page v

Introduction   Page 1
        T.P. WISEMAN

1. Competition and Co-operation   Page 3
        T.P. WISEMAN

2. Politics in the Late Republic   Page 21
        JEREMY PATERSON

3. The Politics of the Early Principate   Page 45
        BARBARA LEVICK

Bibliographical Notes   Page 69

Biographical Notes   Page 77

Index   Page 79

Acknowledgements

The Editor wishes to thank Valerie Harris for her help with word-processing the text and Seán Goddard, who designed the cover.

Chronological Table

B.C.

90-89   War of the Allies ('Social War'): enfranchisement of Italy
88   Sulla consul: march on Rome
86   Death of Marius
83-2   Civil war
82-80   Sulla dictator: proscriptions

80   Pompey's first triumph
79   Death of Sulla
77   Rebellion and death of Lepidus
71   Pompey's second triumph

70   Pompey and Crassus consuls
66   Pompey's command against Mithridates
65   Crassus censor: abortive attempts to annex Egypt
63   Cicero consul: 'conspiracy' of Catalina
61   Pompey's third triumph

60   Alliance of Pompey, Crassus and Caesar ('first triumvirate')
59   Caesar consul
58-7   Exile of Cicero
54   Caesar in Britain and Germany
53   Defeat and death of Crassus at Carrhae

49-5   Civil wars
48   Defeat and murder of Pompey
46   Caesar's triumph
44   Murder of Caesar
43   Octavian consul: triumvirate: murder of Cicero
42-40   Civil wars

38-6   Civil wars
31   Civil war: battle of Actium

30   Fall of Alexandria: suicides of Antony and Cleopatra
29   Octavian's triumph
28   Census: Senate purged
27   Octavian becomes Augustus, given provincial imperium
23   Augustus given tribunician power: conspiracy of Caepio and Murena?

B.C.

19	Augustus' imperium made valid in Rome
18	Senate purged
17	Secular games
13	Tiberius consul
7	Tiberius' first triumph
2	Augustus 'pater patriae': exile of Julia

A.D.

4	Death of C.Caesar: Augustus adopts Tiberius: Senate purged
7	Exile of Agrippa Postumus
8	Exile of Julia II
12	Tiberius' second triumph
14	Death of Augustus: Tiberius princeps
16	Trial and suicide of Libo Drusus
19	Death of Germanicus
20	Trial and suicide of Cn. Piso
23	Death of Drusus
26	Tiberius leaves Rome
29	Exile of Agrippina
31	Consulship and execution of Sejanus
33	Death of Agrippina
37	Death of Tiberius: Gaius princeps: suicide of Ti. Gemellus
39	Execution of Gaetulicus: exile of Agrippina II
41	Murder of Gaius: attempt to restore Republic: Claudius princeps
42	Rebellion and execution of Scribonianus
44	Claudius' triumph
47	Suicide of Valerius Asiaticus
48	Claudius censor: marriage and execution of Silius and Messalina
54	Death of Claudius: Nero princeps
55	Murder of Britannicus
59	Murder of Agrippina II
65	Conspiracy and suicide of C. Piso
67	Suicide of Corbulo
68	Suicide of Nero: Galba princeps
69	Murder of Galba: civil war: Vespasian princeps

Introduction

T.P. WISEMAN

For about five centuries of Rome's existence, we know practically nothing at first hand of her political life. The recently discovered inscription of the 'comrades of Poplius Valesius' gives us a fleeting insight into the archaic warrior aristocracy of the sixth century, and the fragmentary remains of the 'Twelve Tables' law code show us something of early-republican society two generations later. But what passes for the political history of early Rome is the creation of later historians with no means of obtaining an authentic insight into the actual political conditions of the time.

The first Roman historians were at work at the very end of the third century B.C. They were senators, and therefore fully understood the politics of their own time; no doubt they were reasonably reliable interpreters of political history for the previous two or three generations as well, their informants being the now elderly sons and grandsons of the protagonists; but for any period before about 300 B.C. they can have had no really accurate picture of how Roman politics were then conducted. In any case, their works have not survived.

The second century B.C. saw a long succession of senatorial historians, some of consular or even censorial rank, who will certainly have been able to give an authentic − if tendentious − account of recent political history. But their works are lost, though something of their view of politics may come through, at second or third hand, in Livy's 'History of Rome from the Foundation', written at the end of the first century B.C. (The section for the years 218-166 B.C. survives, but Livy's own lack of political experience makes his analysis quite inadequate.) Only with the later second century, when we gradually come within memory-range of the men the young Cicero had talked to, does a really clear picture of Roman political life begin to take shape.

For the politics of the first century, down to 43 B.C., the Ciceronian evidence is of unparalleled richness. There is nothing comparable for the triumviral and Augustan periods, though something can be got from the works of later authors (Velleius, Suetonius, Plutarch, Dio), and epigraphic evidence, especially of career inscriptions, now becomes much fuller and more important. From A.D. 14 onwards, with infuriating gaps at 30-31, 37-47 and 66-68, Tacitus' magnificent 'History of Rome from the Death of Augustus' (commonly called the <u>Annals</u>) provides a detailed political history of the Julian-Claudian period through the eyes of a ferociously intelligent senior senator in the early second century. The <u>Annals</u> are based on good contemporary sources, including the official records of senatorial debates, so even when Tacitus' interpretations are suspect, the information he provides makes possible the reconstruction of political life at a level of detail not far short of that possible for the Ciceronian age.

The chronological limits of this book are therefore those of the usable evidence - essentially, Cicero and Tacitus. But in any case, the period from the War of the Allies to the end of Augustus' dynasty, when considered from the point of view of the ruling class of the Roman Republic, has a real historical unity: it is no accident that names such as Calpurnius Piso, Domitius Ahenobarbus and Iulius Caesar are as important at the end of it as at the beginning. Great changes took place, of course, during those 160 years - in particular the emergence of a single dominant political figure after the civil wars of 49-30 B.C. Even the principate of Augustus, however, did not wholly disrupt the continuity of political life in the Roman oligarchy, and it is that continuity which these studies attempt to illustrate.

1. Competition and Co-operation

T.P. WISEMAN

1. Primus, maximus, optimus

In 221 B.C., L. Caecilius Metellus died, <u>pontifex maximus</u> and the founder of one of the greatest noble houses of the Republic. His son, later to be consul in 205, spoke the funeral oration. The text was preserved, and a quotation from it by the elder Pliny gives us our best insight into the conceptual world of the Roman oligarchy:

> L. Metellus was a <u>pontifex</u>, twice consul, dictator, master of horse, and <u>quindecimvir</u> for the distribution of land; he was the first to lead elephants in a triumphal procession, during the first Punic war. In the funeral oration, his son Q. Metellus wrote: 'He achieved the ten greatest and best things, which wise men spend their whole lives seeking. He wished to be the first of warriors, the best of orators, and the most valiant of commanders; to be in charge of the greatest affairs and held in the greatest honour; to possess supreme wisdom and be regarded as supreme in the Senate; to come to great wealth by honourable means; to leave many children; and to be the most distinguished person in the state. These things he achieved, and none but he achieved them since Rome was founded.'

What is most conspicuous in this precious document of aristocratic values is the use of superlatives - first, best, greatest, and so on. We find the same feature in the earliest of the Scipionic epitaphs - 'This man Lucius Scipio (<u>cos</u>. 259), as most agree, was the very best of all good men at Rome' - and in the inscription copied from the column erected in honour of C. Duilius (<u>cos</u>. 260), who is praised for putting to flight <u>all</u> the <u>greatest</u>

Carthaginian forces and for being the _first_ to fight a successful sea battle. It was clearly important to these men not only to achieve glory, but to be seen to surpass all their rivals in doing so. (1)

The moment when a Roman knew he was first, best and greatest was when he rode in the triumphal chariot to make his dedication to Jupiter the Best and Greatest, whose appearance and attributes he had himself taken on for that day. But it was only for a day: how could the glory be made to last? By statues, paintings, inscriptions, and above all by the use of the captured booty (_manubiae_) to build a temple or other 'monument'. The word itself tells us what such a building was – a permanent and visible 'reminder' (_monimentum_) of the achievement which had made its construction possible. (2) By such means the _triumphator_ could overcome the fact that his moment of glory was not permanent. His other problem was that it was not unique. Other men triumphed, other men built _monimenta_ with their _manubiae_. It is no doubt for this reason that the Duilius inscription insisted on the exact number of ships sunk and the exact quantity of booty captured – objective proof that his triumph was the best.

In a society where personal glory mattered so much, disputes about who was really entitled to it must have been frequent. One way they could be resolved was by the challenge of a 'legal wager' (_sponsione provocare_), as when A. Calatinus adjudicated between the praetor Q. Valerius Falto and the consul C. Lutatius Catulus as to who had really won the battle of the Aegates Islands in 242. It was simply a formalised version of the natural and inevitable way of settling questions of honour in an aristocratic society with agreed standards of excellence, namely appeal to the accepted opinion of one's peers. That was certainly the criterion by which the men we know of justified the superlatives they applied to themselves: 'most Romans agreed' on the pre-eminence of L. Scipio, and L. Metellus 'was regarded as' the chief senator. (3)

This preoccupation with personal achievement and competition for the greatest glory, which stands out as the most conspicuous characteristic of the Roman ruling class in the third century B.C., can be traced right through the history of the middle and late Republic and into the early Empire.

Some of the best examples come from _tabulae triumphales_ – inscriptions attached to temples or other monuments, recording in archaic Saturnian metre the exploits of the _triumphator_. Two complete examples (L. Aemilius Regillus _pr_. 190 and Ti. Sempronius Gracchus _cos_. 177) are reported by Livy, though the text is very uncertain; stray lines from two others (M'. Acilius Glabrio _cos_. 191, and one unattributed) are quoted in treatises on Roman metre; and fragments of one more (C. Sempronius Tuditanus _cos_. 129) survive at the Latin colony of Aquileia at the head of the Adriatic. (4) This is what they say:

> (i) When Lucius Aemilius the son of Marcus went out to battle to put an end to a great war and to subdue kings ... under his auspicious command and fortunate leadership the fleet of Antiochus, ever before invincible, was defeated, shattered and put to flight between Ephesus, Samos and Chios, before the very eyes of Antiochus and of his whole army, his cavalry and elephants. On that day, forty-two ships of war were captured there with all their crews; and after that battle had been fought, King Antiochus and his realm [were brought into the power of the Roman People (?)] ...

> (ii) Under the auspices and command of the consul Tiberius Sempronius Gracchus, the legions and army of the Roman People subjugated Sardinia. In that province 80,000 of the enemy were either killed or taken prisoner. He did his public duty with the greatest success, freed our allies, restored our revenues, and brought his army home safe and sound and laden with booty. For the second time he entered Rome in triumph...

> (iii) He defeated, put to flight and destroyed the greatest legions.

> (iv) ... who smashed the greatest royal power of kings.

> (v) ... four times in fifteen days he defeated and put to flight the Taurisci and Carni and the Liburni, whom he drove from the seas to the shores. Outstanding in the success of his standards and his strategy, Tuditanus therefore held a triumph at Rome ...

Felicissume, maximas, summas, praecipuos - the boastful superlatives recur in the familiar way, with the extra second-century dimension provided by royal adversaries. Men who put kings to flight are clearly greater than kings themselves.

But what if you did not have the opportunity to defeat kings or barbarian peoples? Here is T. Annius Rufus (cos. 128), as his achievements appeared beneath his statue at Annius' Forum on

Annius' Road: (5)

> I made the road from Regium to Capua and on that
> road I placed all the bridges, milestones and
> inscriptions. From here there are 51 miles to
> Nuceria, 84 to Capua, 74 to Muranum, 123 to
> Consentia, 180 to Valentia, 231 to the Strait at
> the statue, 237 to Regium. Total from Capua to
> Regium, 321. And I also as praetor in Sicily
> sought out the runaway slaves belonging to Italians
> and brought back 917 men. I also was the first to
> cause herdsmen to give way to ploughmen on the
> public land. I built the market and public
> buildings here.

If you can't enumerate enemy casualties, miles of road will have to
do. But enumeration of some sort is essential, to make it clear
how great your achievement has been. So it was in the Duilius
inscription a century earlier, so it is again a century later in
the records of Pompey's triumph, or in the res gestae inscription
of Augustus himself. (6)

> Annius' inscription, like the contemporary Scipionic
epitaphs that explain what the dead man would have achieved if he
had had the chance, shows us how necessary it was for all Roman
senators, and not just the victorious commanders, to stake their
claim for glory. Men who to us appear as very minor characters in
the historical record portray themselves as paragons of heroic
valour. This is demonstrated most revealingly by a Latin elegiac
poem set up at the Isthmus of Corinth by a certain Lucilius Hirrus,
the first senator of his family known to us, probably in 102 B.C.:
(7)

> Learn of a exploit no-one has ever attempted or dared(?)
>   that we may bear a hero's deeds in honour.
> A fleet under proconsul Marcus Antonius' auspices
>   was brought across the isthmus and put to sea.
> He himself set out for Sida; Hirrus the propraetor
>   stationed the fleet at Athens because of the season.
> This was achieved in a few days with little trouble,
>   accompanied by sound sense and safe deliverance.
> He who is upright praises, he who is not is envious;
>   let them envy, provided they see how seemly the deed (?).

A legate under another man's command sees to the safe transport of
a naval squadron over the Isthmus and into harbour: granted that it
was done 'with little trouble', the achievement hardly seems to
merit the somewhat hysterical praise with which Hirrus' client-
poet has invested it. The last couplet betrays the reason - the
competition a man had to face in making his career. (Not

surprisingly, despite the poet's efforts, this particular heroic achievement did not suffice to bring Hirrus to the consulship.)

That competitive instinct, that urge to be first and greatest, is all too easily recognisable in the last generation of the Roman Republic. We need only think of Pompeius Magnus, the Roman Alexander, who triumphed at 24 and became consul without ever holding any previous magistracy; of M. Crassus, his rival, who hoped to add Egypt to the Roman empire, and met his death against the Parthians trying to put Pompey's achievements in the shade; of C. Caesar, the first to lead Roman armies beyond the Rhine and the Channel, whose talent, ruthlessness and luck eventually brought him to the logical conclusion of the urge to be first – the position, and the fate, of a quasi-monarch. According to a credible report in Suetonius, even before the civil war Caesar used to dwell on his position as princeps civitatis: 'it's harder to push me down from first place to second than from second to last'. It mattered, who was first and who was second.

It would be a mistake to think that only the 'big three' felt like that, or that such feelings became obsolete with the Ides of March. The year after the deaths of Cleopatra and Antony, the man Octavian had left in command of Egypt set up a trilingual inscription on the island of Philae, below the first cataract of the Nile:

> C. Cornelius Gallus son of Gnaeus, Roman knight, first prefect of Alexandria and Egypt after the overthrow of the monarchy by Caesar the son of the Deified Julius, having been victorious in two pitched battles in fifteen days ...; having led his army beyond the Nile cataract, a region into which arms had not previously been carried either by the Roman People or by the kings of Egypt; having subjugated the Thebaid, the common terror of them all,... dedicated this offering to the ancestral gods and to the Nile, his ally.

That was too much, especially as Gallus recorded his achievements on the Pyramids as well. He was recalled in disgrace and killed himself. (9) It was not for the new Caesar's agents to vaunt themselves so.

For Augustus himself, of course, the traditional boastful pride was wholly appropriate, and his trophy at La Turbie (6 B.C.) duly enumerated the Alpine peoples conquered 'under his leadership and auspices.' It was appropriate for his heirs too. The Portico of Gaius and Lucius in the Roman Forum carried a splendid dedicatory inscription, of which enough survives for us to be sure of the message:

> The Senate and People of Rome to C. Caesar, son of
> Augustus, grandson of the deified Julius, Prince of
> Youth, pontifex, consul designate. He was the
> first of all to be created consul at 14 years of
> age.

And above all, the res gestae inscription set up before Augustus'
mausoleum conspicuously attests the survival of the traditional
ideals, quantifying the details of his benefactions and insisting
on the uniqueness of his achievements. (10)

The princeps was inevitably pre-eminent, so it was only to
be expected that he and his heirs should inherit the ideals and
phraseology of the great men of the past. What is much more
significant is that the descendants and successors of those great
men continued to think the same way too. As Dr. Levick's chapter
in this book makes clear, their life was as competitive as ever,
and the prizes were not much smaller. There were no triumphs any
more, except for the princeps and his relatives; but triumphal
decorations could be won by imperial legates, and pride in
achievement was still celebrated in an uneasy combination of
personal glory and loyalty to the emperor. The two examples that
follow are from fragmentary inscriptions plausibly attributed to M.
Vinicius and L. Piso, consuls in 19 and 15 B.C. respectively:

> ... propraetorian legate of Augustus Caesar in
> Illyricum, was the first to lead an army (?) across
> the river Danube into the territory of the ... and
> the Bastarnae ... and he put to flight the Cotini
> and the Anartii ...

> ... the king; when it was brought into the control
> of Imperator Caesar Augustus and the Roman People,
> the Senate decreed to the immortal gods a double
> thanksgiving for deeds well done, and to (the
> legate) himself triumphal decorations ...

Aristocratic funeral orations still dwelt on the familiar themes,
such as L. Ahenobarbus' venture further into Germany than any Roman
general had gone before; honorary statues, in consular and
triumphal dress, were still sought after and lovingly recorded, as
the recently discovered inscription of L. Volusius Saturninus
spectacularly reveals. (11) It was a long way from calling oneself
optimus or maximus in the third-century manner, but it was
recognisably the same tradition.

In one sense, the history of the Julio-Claudians is the
history of the slow extinction of this tradition. The extinction
was inevitable, since ultimately an ethos of personal

aggrandisement could not co-exist with devotion to the princeps;
the surprising thing is how long it took to come about. A visitor
to the temple of Venus on Mt. Eryx in Sicily in Tiberius' reign
would have found the transitional nature of that period strikingly
illustrated by two statues and a trophy that had been dedicated to
the goddess. They were set up by L. Apronius Caesianus (later cos.
A.D. 39) in honour of his father L. Apronius (cos. A.D. 8), one of
the great men of his time. The inscription, with two couplets for
each item, runs as follows:

> The son of Apronius, greater in deeds than in name
>   because he himself put to flight the Gaetulian tribes,
> has set up, goddess, the statue of his dear father
>   (a fair reward to you, gentle mother of Aeneas' sons),
> and also the arms he wore; in this shield broken with blows
>   what valour is revealed! The sword is red from the foe
> and worn with slaughter; the trophy is crowned by the spear
>   that struck the fierce savage in the face and felled him.
> No statue is more revered by either than this,
>   which father and son have dedicated to you:
> the equal affection of both has set up Caesar's likeness.
>   They competed in dutifulness, which excelled in each.

A man of Apronius' stature could have his own virtus extolled in
the old way, but even he had to link it with pietas towards the
emperor. (12)

The same ambiguity appears in a more acute form in the
tomb inscriptions of Q. Veranius (cos. A.D. 49) — his own
achievements are set out in detail, but with heavy emphasis on the
authority of Claudius and Nero — and of Ti. Plautius Silvanus
Aelianus (cos. A.D. 45 and 74), whose account of his res gestae as
imperial legate of Moesia under Nero contained phrases the men of
the second century B.C. would have recognised:

> to the bank which he protected (i.e. the Danube) he
> brought kings unknown before, or hostile to the
> Roman People, to pay homage to the Roman standards
> ... he was the first to relieve the food supply of
> the Roman People with a great quantity of corn from
> that province ...

But Vespasian's authority for his triumphal decorations and
prefecture of the city is emphasised at the end, with a verbatim
quotation from the emperor's honorific speech. (13)

It was well observed by A.R. Burn, in a quite different
context, that it usually takes two or three generations 'for a
people, after a far-reaching social change, to get habits which are
no longer relevant thoroughly out of their system; for the first
generation of survivors are still people brought up under the old

order, and the second generation are people brought up by people who were brought up under the old order'. (14) It is probably not a coincidence that the republican ruling class as we know it first becomes articulate about the time of the first Punic war, just a century after the Licinio-Sextian laws had broken the patrician monopoly of office; nor that the last manifestations of their way of life appear under the emperor Vespasian, just a century after the transactions of 27, 23 and 19 B.C. had finally transformed the Republic into the Principate.

2.   The heroic ethos

I have deliberately restricted the discussion to first-hand evidence, what Roman politicians said of themselves. But that may still be misleading: funerary orations and honorific inscriptions were for public consumption, and the value system they reveal could be merely conventional, of no greater significance for the realities of life than are the references to 'right honourable gentlemen' in the British Parliament. Was the competitive tradition of personal achievement a real motive in political decision-making? As it happens, we have the best possible evidence – the private correspondence of Cicero – that in the last years of the Republic it was a real and vital influence on at least one man's behaviour.

Cicero writes to Atticus in December of 60 B.C. The alliance of Pompey, Crassus and Caesar is just being formed; Cicero has to decide whether to put up an honourable resistance to their planned agrarian law, or to give himself a tranquil and popular old age by helping its passage against his principles, or to avoid the issue by retiring ingloriously to the country. How does he resolve the dilemma, in this private letter to the confidant of all his plans? By appeal to the standards of heroic poetry, his own and Homer's:

> I can't forget my finale in Book III:
> 'Meantime the paths which thou from earliest days did seek,
> Aye, and when Consul too, as mood and virtue bade,
> These hold, and foster still thy fame and good men's praise.'
> Such was Calliope's own lesson to me in a book which
> contains many aristocratic sentiments. So I don't
> think I can hestitate. I must always find
> 'One omen best: to fight for fatherland.'

If we find it startling that Cicero should borrow the words used by Hector before he went out to fight, that is only a failure of imagination on our part. For a man who had made his career by his own merits against tough opposition, it came naturally to think of Homer's heroes at critical moments. (15)

In April 59, tempted by Caesar's offer of a state mission to Alexandria, he answers in Hector's words again: 'I fear the Trojans and their long-gowned wives'. Thinking of what history would say of him in a thousand years, he chooses the gloria of rejecting Caesar's bounty as if it were the acceptance of Achilles' challenge. As a boy, Cicero had loved Peleus' advice to the young Achilles, 'Far to excel, out-topping all the rest', as we discover from his bitter resentment at the loss of that ideal under the renewed domination of the 'triumvirs' in 54: he cannot attack his enemies, and must sometimes even defend them. And at the greatest crisis of all, as Pompey prepares to abandon Italy to Caesar in March 49, Cicero reflects on what he owes to Pompey as if he were the doomed Achilles remembering Patroclus:

> I think of how in Homer a mother and a goddess says to
> her son
>   'Thy doom awaits thee after Hector's end'.
> And her son replies
>   'Let me die quickly, since my friend is slain
>   And I not there to aid'.

There are some responsibilities for which one must be prepared to give one's life. (16)

It is perfectly true that we must allow for self-dramatisation, and recognise that Cicero's performance was not usually as heroic as his resolve; but the fact remains that the Roman Republic was an aristocratic society in which the motivation of the principes could be expressed without absurdity in Homeric terms.

That becomes clear in an interesting letter of 45 B.C., where Cicero expresses his acquiescence in the dictatorship as the abandonment of 'Homeric magniloquence'. He explains to Caesar why, with ultimately disastrous consequences to himself, he had refused to join him in 59:

> For I could hear our nobles shouting
>   'Be valiant and win praise from men unborn'.
>   So spake he, and dark clouds of woe fell on him.
> Nevertheless they still try to console me: even now
> they want a man already singed to go up in a blaze of
> glory, crying
>   'Nay, die not meanly and all unrenowned,
>   But do a deed posterity shall hear'.
> But as you see, I take less notice of them now. So
> I turn aside from Homer's sublimities to the true
> precepts of Euripides:
>   'I hate advisers ill-advised themselves'.

Urged to glory by the aristocrats as Telemachus was by Athene, Cicero comes in exile to the black despair of Laertes. And now they are urging him again, as Hector, to go out against Achilles, with the same promised reward - fame among posterity for his res gestae. Even now that he rejects such dangerous heroics, Cicero still goes on to wonder whether a man can look out for his own safety and yet continue to 'excel the rest', in the words of Peleus that evidently still haunted him. (17)

So it was real to them, and not just a convention. 'Ever excel, out-topping all the rest' could have been a motto for any of the great men of the Republic, summing up as it does not only the Homeric ethos but also the aristocratic ideal of personal achievement in the Roman ruling class.

A society based on the pursuit of honour, whether Homeric kleos or Roman gloria, is bound to be competitive. As Professor Walcot succinctly put it, 'the man of honour is anxious to promote his own honour at the expense of the honour of others. There is only a limited amount of honour at hand, and one resents and envies the possession of it by other people.' Cicero was certainly conscious of the envy (invidia) his contemporaries felt towards him, and we have seen Lucilius Hirrus challenging it in the last couplet of his inscription at the Isthmus. (18) The invidi were those one had outstripped in the competition.

One of the most revealing commentators on late-republican political life is the poet-philosopher Lucretius. From his detached Epicurean viewpoint he saw his fellow-citizens

> competing in strife of talent or noble birth
> struggling night and day with surpassing effort
> to get to the summit of riches and power over things.
> O miserable minds of men, blind hearts ...
> Men have wished to be famous and powerful, so that
> their fortune might rest on a firm foundation
> and themselves live a peaceful life in enjoyment of riches -
> but all in vain. For in striving to reach the summit
> of honour, they have made their own way dangerous;
> even from the top, like lightning, contemptuous envy
> frequently casts them down to the foul abyss.
> For envy, like lightning, usually strikes the highest
> and sets on fire whatever stands out from the rest.

The first thing to observe is the importance of riches. Like Horace in the next generation, and the love-elegists with their consciously anti-heroic ethos, who equated military adventure with avarice, Lucretius takes it for granted that the pursuit of glory is also the pursuit of wealth. (19) The victorious general had the legal right to the spoil of his victory, and though he was expected to deliver a substantial proportion to the public

treasury, and distribute appropriate rewards to his officers and
men, what was left might make him, quite legitimately, a wealthy
man. The same applied to the profits of a peacful <u>provincia</u>:
without breaking any laws, Cicero was over two million sesterces
better off after his year as proconsul of Cilicia; less scrupulous
governors could of course amass many times that amount. (20)

From L. Metellus in 205 B.C. (p.3 above) to L. Volusius
Saturninus in A.D. 56, the eulogies at aristocratic funerals dwelt
on 'wealth honourably gained' as a natural part of the achievement
of glory. Its place in the scheme of things may be seen in the
'Second Letter to Caesar' ascribed to Sallust – probably the work
of an early-imperial rhetorician, but no less valuable for that as
evidence for the continuity of aristocratic ideology: (21)

> If your country and your ancestors could speak to
> you, they would say this, I think: 'Caesar, we who
> are the bravest of men have sired you in a most
> excellent city, to be our glory and our protection
> and to strike terror into our foes. What we won
> with much toil and peril we gave you together with
> your life when you were born: a country without
> rival on earth, a house and family most illustrious
> in that country, excellent accomplishments, riches
> honestly gained, in fact all the adornments of
> peace and profits of war.'

The main point of Lucretius' diatribe, however, is the
idea of struggle – '<u>certare</u> ingenio, <u>contendere</u> nobilitate'. The
man in public life is forever striving, competing. Lucilius the
satirist in the second century B.C., and Varro, Lucretius and
Horace in the first, all found those two verbs the natural
expressions to use in describing Roman politics. (22) They knew
their society much more intimately than we ever can, and we must
take their description seriously.

3. <u>Factions and family groups</u>

It is basic, then, that Roman politics were competitive.
Of course – but historians often write as if they had forgotten it,
and emphasise co-operation rather than competition. Mercifully, we
no longer hear much of those imaginary entities the 'popular party'
and the 'senatorial party' which loomed so large in nineteenth-
century political histories of Rome. But 'factions', which have
taken their place, and on which much modern analysis of Roman
republican politics depends, were also essentially co-operative in
nature: can they really have formed the normal stuff of politics at
Rome?

It is important to remember that <u>factio</u> is inevitably a
pejorative word. Nonius Marcellinus defined it in his dictionary

as 'the unanimity and agreement of bad men', and Sallust observed
that a combination of politicians based on common aims or fears was
'friendship among good men, _factio_ among bad'. 'Bad men' means
more than just 'political opponents'. It has an objective sense:
men who use their co-operation for unjust ends incompatible with
the laws and the common good. The Catilinarian conspirators were a
factio; so, according to Calvus and Cicero, was the alliance of
Pompey, Crassus and Caesar in the fifties. But such groups were a
perversion of Roman politics, not the norm. (23)

      At one level, of course, there _was_ co-operation. The
Roman Senate was no doubt quite familiar _with_ the sort of scene
Seneca attributes to the Olympian one:

          Hercules, who saw that his own iron was in the
          fire, was running about this way and that saying
          'Don't refuse me, it's important to me. Anything
          you want afterwards I'll do for you in return.
          Scratch my back, I'll scratch yours.'

Quintus Cicero's <u>Short Guide to Electioneering</u> is full of the
mutual promise and performance of favours to get things done (in
that case to deliver the vote at the consular elections), but that
did not make Cicero and his supporters _factiosi_. 'Do this for me
and I'll do that for you' is not at all the same as 'Let the two of
us work together to pursue our joint interest'. A Roman politician
was expected to look out for the interests of himself and his
family; it was his duty to look out for the common interests of the
Senate and People of Rome, or at least of 'all good men' in the
moral sense of 'good' as most Romans understood it; but to look out
for the interests of any intermediate group was to be part of a
cabal (_factio paucorum_). (24) It is a mistake to assume that this
third procedure formed the regular conduct of Roman public life: to
call all political friendships factions makes it impossible to
distinguish the real _factiones_ when they appear.

      What has led scholars into this trap, I think, is a
failure of the visual imagination. One distinguished historian,
for instance, uses 'faction' to mean 'an assemblage of individuals
and families co-operating for mutual political advantage'. (25)
The mind boggles at _families_ assembling, but even if we concentrate
on the individuals we still need to ask the practical question,
where and under what circumstances did they meet?

      There is an interesting passage in Vitruvius' archi-
tectural handbook, where he discusses the sorts of house
appropriate to various types of occupier. For aristocrats with
public duties to perform, the architect must provide not only halls
and peristyles of suitable grandeur but also libraries and
basilicas comparable to public buildings, 'because in their houses
public _consilia_ and private _iudicia_ and _arbitria_ are carried out'.

There was only a limited amount of space in even the most sumptuous town house, but the sort of thing Vitruvius meant can be illustrated by the large central room, flanked by libraries, in the 'house of Augustus' excavated in 1961 at the western corner of the Palatine. (26)

What were the meetings referred to by Vitruvius? 'Public consilia' were the advisory councils which Roman magistrates were expected to consult before taking important action. 'Private iudicia and arbitria' were hearings of civil law suits delegated by the praetor; there too it was normal for the iudex or arbiter to be assisted by a body of advisers. And we can add a further activity not mentioned by Vitruvius: when in his domestic role a Roman had to decide on important questions of filial discipline, manumission and the like, he called a family council to advise him, and presumably used the same 'committee room' as for his public and legal duties. (27)

I suspect that it was not only in his capacity as magistrate, judicial arbiter or paterfamilias that a Roman statesman used such rooms for consultation. Whenever he was faced with a difficult political issue, it would surely seem natural to him to invite those he could trust to discuss the matter and advise him. The important point is that one man invited the others. We are imagining not (normally) the meeting of a cabal, but an individual taking advice on how he should perform his own duties – which included duties to the res publica, to his family and dependants, to his ancestors, to those who had done him favours in the past, and so on. (28)

There is no shortage of evidence for such meetings. The setting of Cicero's de oratore shows us L. Crassus calling his advisers to his villa at Tusculum to discuss the political situation in the autumn of 91 B.C., before he delivered the great senatorial speech that turned out to be his swan-song. In Plutarch's Life of Cicero we see the consul of 63 B.C., on the evening of 4 December, discussing with his brother and his friends the next day's senatorial debate on the fate of the conspirators. Cicero's own correspondence reports the meeting at Brutus' villa at Antium a few weeks after the Ides of March, when Cassius, Cicero and others were summoned to join Brutus' own relatives in advising him whether or not to return to Rome and face Antony. Those occasions happened to be unusually dramatic, but the procedure was normal. (29)

It is worth noticing that some of the groups modern historians identify are easier to imagine in these practical terms than others. We can visualise the 'Catonian group' without difficulty – the men Cato will habitually have called as his advisers – but not, I think, the 'Metellan faction', except in the sense (which is not what modern historians usually mean) of the friends and advisers of a particular Metellus at a particular time. The significant unit in Roman politics was not the family, not the 'group', but the individual. That was inherent in the competitive structure of senatorial life and the 'heroic' ideology of being first, best and greatest.

However, the number of important individuals was limited. It was not every single senator whose views one had to reckon with, as we can see from Cicero's correspondence. The opinions that mattered were those of the ex-consuls, the men of authority, the men who made speeches in the Senate and not those who just said 'I agree with so-and-so' or voted with their feet by walking across the floor of the House. Nor do we have to imagine an ad hoc decision on every separate issue as it arose. The nucleus, at least, of a senior senator's consilium would be more or less constant, and a certain continuity of collective opinion no doubt emerged. Moreover, the continuity could go back a generation or more, for a man's ancestors were his advisers too. In a society where mos maiorum mattered so much, Roman politics were not completely fragmented. We must not over-emphasise the uniqueness of the individual.

Cicero's political analyses in his letters do talk about specific influential men and their attitudes, but also about 'the good men' (boni) as a collective noun. The boni were not a faction in any useful sense of the term. They were simply the men Cicero regarded as sound, who could be depended on to respect tradition, play the game by the accepted rules and resist radical change. It was a way of thinking natural to many Roman senators – so natural that on many issues it did make sense to talk about what the boni thought, and to define the opinions of heterodox individuals by how much they differed from the common view. But there were no 'parties', no 'groups of families', and 'factions' only to the extent that the system was sometimes deliberately perverted. If we want to understand the machinery of decision-making in the Roman Republic (and, mutatis mutandis, in the early Principate as well), we must try to reconstruct what a particular Roman statesman is likely to have had in his mind when he sat down with the men he could trust and asked their advice about a particular political issue.

Notes

1.   Pliny, <u>Nat</u>. <u>Hist</u>. VII 139–140; <u>ILLRP</u> 310, 319 = E.H. Warmington, <u>Remains of Old Latin</u> IV (Loeb Classical Library 1940) 4–5, 128–131. See also Livy XXXIX 40 on M. Cato, esp. 40.6: 'in bello manu fortissimus...summus imperator; idem in pace...peritissimus...eloquentissimus', etc.

2.   Jupiter: H.S.Versnel, <u>Triumphus</u> (Leiden 1970) 56–93; S.Weinstock, <u>Divus Julius</u> (Oxford 1971) 67–75. <u>Monumenta</u>: Festus 123L, 'monimentum est...quicquid ob memoriam alicuius factum est, ut fana, porticus, scripta et carmina'; Cic. <u>ad fam</u>. I 9.15, <u>in Verr</u>. IV 69, etc.

3.   <u>Sponsione provocare</u>: John Crook, <u>JRS</u> 66 (1976) 132–8; cf. Cic. <u>de off</u>. III 77, A. Gellius XIV 2.26 on <u>sponsiones</u> 'whether X is a good man' or 'a better man than Y'. Calatinus: Val. Max. II 8.2.

4.   Livy XL 52.5–6, XLI 28.8–10; <u>Gramm.Lat</u>. (ed. Keil) VI 265, 293f; <u>ILLRP</u> 335 = Warmington <u>132–3</u>, with improved text by M.G.Morgan, <u>Philologus</u> 117 (1973) 40–48.

5.   <u>ILLRP</u> 454 = Warmington 150–1, with T.P.Wiseman, <u>PBSR</u> 32 (1964) 30–37 and 37 (1969) 88–91.

6.   Pompey: Diodorus XL 4, Plutarch <u>Pompey</u> 45, Appian <u>Mithridatica</u> 117. Augustus: <u>Res Gestae</u> (trans. and commentary by P.A.Brunt and J.M.Moore, Oxford 1967), esp. sections 3–4, 8, 15–18, 21–25.

7.   <u>ILLRP</u> 342 = Warmington 132–5, with S.Dow, <u>HSCP</u> 60 (1951) 81–100. For the Scipionic epitaphs, see <u>ILLRP</u> 311–6 = Warmington 4–9.

8.   Suet. <u>Caes</u>. 29.1. Cf. also Caes. <u>BC</u> I 4.4 on Pompey: 'neminem dignitate secum exaequari volebat'.

9.   <u>ILS</u> 8995 = Ehrenberg and Jones, <u>Documents</u> (see p.73 below) 21; Dio LIII 23.5 for the Pyramids.

10.   Trophy: Pliny <u>Nat</u>. <u>Hist</u>. III 136–7 = Ehrenberg and Jones 40. Portico: <u>CIL</u> VI 36893. <u>Res Gestae</u> (n.6 above): 10.2 'never before', 12.1 'no-one but me', 16.1 'first and only', 26.4 'no-one before', 31.1 'never before', 32.3 'never before',

34.3 'I excelled all ...'. For the traditional values applied
in the imperial family, see also the Consolatio ad Liviam
(text and trans. in the Loeb volume entitled Ovid, Art of Love
and Other Poems), esp. lines 451-466, and the inscription of
Claudius' triumphal arch (ILS 216 = Smallwood, Documents (see
p.73 below) 43b), on which see D.R.Dudley, Birmingham Univ.
Hist. Journ. 7 (1959) 9-13.

11. Piso and Vinicius: ILS 918, 8965 = Ehrenberg and Jones 199,
     43a, with R.Syme, Danubian Papers (Bucharest 1971) 32f, 35,
     65f. Ahenobarbus: Tac. Ann. IV 44.3. Volusius Saturninus:
     JRS 61 (1971) 143.

12. ILS 939: see Tac. Ann. III 21 on Apronius and his son in
     Africa in A.D. 20.

13. Veranius: Smallwood 231c. Aelianus: ILS 986 = Smallwood 228.

14. A.R.Burn, The Traveller's History of Greece (London 1965) 43.
     Cf. Tac. Ann. I 1.

15. Cic. ad Att. II 3.3-4, quoting his own poem 'On my Consulship'
     and Iliad XII 243 (Hector).

16. Cic. ad Att. II 5.1, quoting Iliad XXII 105, XII 100 (both
     Hector); ad Q.f. III 5.4, quoting Iliad XI 784 (Peleus to
     Achilles); ad Att. IX 5.3, quoting Iliad XVIII 94 (Thetis) and
     96-7 (Achilles).

17. Cic. ad fam. XIII 15. 1-2, quoting Odyssey I 302 (Athena to
     Telemachus), XXIV 315 (Laertes), Iliad XXII 304-5 (Hector),
     Euripides frag. 905N.

18. Peter Walcot, Greece and Rome 20 (1973) 117. Cicero: ad Att.
     I 19.6, 20.3, II 1.7, 9.2, 19.4, IV 1.8, 3.5, 5.2; ad fam. I
     7.7-8.

19. Lucr. II 10-14, V 1120-8 (cf. also III 59-64, 74-78, 995-
     1003). Avarice: Lucr. III 59, Hor. Ars poet. 167, Odes I 29;
     Tibullus I 1 (cf. also I 2.67-72, II 3.39-42), Propertius III
     4, etc.

20. Cic. ad fam. V 20.9. General's right to booty: I. Shatzman,
     Historia 21 (1972) 177-205.

21. Volusius: Tac. Ann. XIII 30.4 (cf. IV 44.1, Cn. Lentulus in
     A.D. 26). Caesar: 'Sall.' ep. Caes. 2.13, trans. J.M.Carter,
     LACTOR no. 6 (London 1970) 45.

22. Lucilius 1228-34M = E.H.Warmington, Remains of Old Latin III
     (Loeb Classical Library 1938) 372f; Varro Menippean Satires

450B, 'et petere imperium populi et contendere honores';
Lucr. II 11, V 1124; Hor. Odes III 1.13.

23. Nonius 473L, Sall. Jug. 31.14. Catilinarians: Sall. Cat.
32.2. Alliance: Calvus in Vatinium frag. 26M (quoted in
Rhetores Latini 366), 'hominem nostrae civitatis audacissimum,
de factione divitem, sordidum, maledicum accuso'; Cic. ad Att.
VII 9.4.

24. Q. Cic. Commentariolum petitionis; trans. D.W.Taylor and
J.Murrell, LACTOR No. 3 (London 1968). Factio paucorum: Caes.
Bell. civ. I 22.5, Hirtius Bell. Gall. VIII 50.2, Sall. Jug.
27.2.

25. E.S.Gruen, Roman Politics and the Criminal Courts 149-78 B.C.
(Harvard 1968) 5.

26. Vitr. Arch. VI 5.2; A.G.McKay, Houses, Villas and Palaces in
the Roman World (London 1975) 70-72, room o in fig. 25a.

27. Advisory councils: e.g. Asconius 89C, 'L. Volcacius Tullus
consul consilium publicum habuit an rationem Catilinae habere
deberet, si peteret consulatum'; see J.Crook, Consilium
Principis (Cambridge 1955) 4-8. Civil law hearings: e.g. Cic.
pro Rosc. com. 12, pro Quinct. 5, 36, 91. Family councils:
e.g. Val. Max. V 9.1, VI 3.7-8; Cic. pro Cluent. 176, pro
Cael. 68.

28. Compare Cicero's regular reports to Atticus on status rei p.
and status meus (each important as a criterion of conduct):
Att. I 16.6 and 11, 18.2, 19.5-6, 20.2-3, II 1.6, 3.3-4, etc.

29. Crassus: Cic. de or. I 26. Cicero: Plut. Cic. 19. Brutus:
Cic. ad Att. XV 11.1.

2. Politics in the Late Republic

JEREMY PATERSON

1. Introduction

It is a widely-held misconception, and one which is actively promoted by politicians, that statesmen relish a crisis. Nothing could be further from the truth. In the hurly-burly of every-day politics the rules of the game are clearly established; the consequences of work or action can be judged finely to promote one's career; due deference can be expected for ancestry, wealth, influence and even for talent. On the other hand in a crisis decisions have to be made in circumstances of murky uncertainty. Much depends on the outcome. Guess wrong, pick a loser, then farewell to career, status, property, even life.

The lives of the last generation of politicians of the Roman Republic were framed by two great crises. The first was the decade between the tribunate of M. Livius Drusus in 91 B.C., and the dictatorship of Sulla, a time which was marked by the marching and counter-marching of armies, by confusion, by muddled loyalties, and by harsh reckonings meted out to opponents. It was difficult to chart a safe course for a political career through such times. The rights and wrongs of the situation were impossible to untangle. As Cicero, a young contemporary, commented much later: 'it might be argued that Sulla or Marius or Cinna had right on their side; perhaps even legality. But what ever was there more cruel or deadly than their victories?' (1)

The perils of these years were seared upon the minds of the survivors and dominated their political thinking. It was inevitable that memories would be stirred in that second great crisis which Julius Caesar precipitated in 49 B.C. by his refusal to come home and meekly face the destruction of his career in the courts. Once again the Roman aristocrats were forced to make choices. 'Quid agam?' ('What am I to do?') is a constant theme in the letters of Cicero at this time. (2) It was easy to find disturbing parallels from forty years earlier. (3) The factors which weighed with men in their decisions were various. Some may have been moved by principle, an amor rei publicae, a greater number by loyalty and obligation to one or other of the protagonists. Despite Cicero's ties with both Caesar and Pompey, his profound debt of gratitude to Pompey largely settled the matter. But even with Cicero another consideration can be discerned. His spell as governor of Cilicia had opened up unexpectedly the possibility of that supreme accolade, a triumph. In all the upheaval Cicero kept part of his mind on the problem of how and from whom he was most likely to obtain this ultimate honour. In this he differed but little from the majority whose own future careers were uppermost in their minds. (4) They would have agreed with M. Caelius Rufus, Cicero's correspondent, that 'as long as the struggle is a political one without resort to arms, a man ought to take the more honourable side; when it comes to fighting, he should choose the stronger and equate the safer course with the better'.

Although it is easy to be shocked by such cynicism, it is important to remember that the civil war which broke out in 49 B.C. was not a clash between great principles, as some modern interpretations suggest. Caesar crossed the Rubicon simply to save his skin and to defend his dignitas, the position which he had gained in Roman public life, not to bring some new political system or panacea to an ailing republic. While many of the Roman aristocracy might disapprove of his methods, most would recognise his goal. What they wanted for themselves was not so different. In the turmoil each sought to promote or to defend the position, wealth and influence which he had managed to build up. (5)

It was personalities not policies which counted for most in the political world of the Late Republic. In his attempt to dramatize the danger of Catiline, Cicero sought to represent him as an anarchist who was bent on the destruction of the whole system. In a vivid and tendentious passage Catiline's perverse ambition is contrasted unfavourably with the aims of those who had been engaged in the civil wars of the 80s: 'the purpose of those disturbances was not to destroy the res publica, but to change it. The men involved did not want there to be no res publica at all, but rather that they should be the leading men (principes) in the res publica which was to continue to exist. They did not want to burn down this city, but rather to flourish within it.' (6) Cicero saw with far greater clarity than many modern historians precisely what was at stake in the political struggles of the last century B.C.

2. 'The Class of 81' – Sulla's men

The aristocrats who came to the fore in the last decades of the Republic could be dubbed aptly 'the Class of 81'. They owed their careers very largely to the return of Sulla and his political settlement in 81 B.C. Many of them had had bitter experience of what it was to be deprived of access to influence and office earlier in their lives. For them Sulla offered the opportunity to get back into public life.

C. Scribonius Curio is a good example. His father, for all his talents, had failed to make it to the consulship, and his death while Curio was still very young probably explains why Curio never had a formal education and rhetorical training. Nevertheless, he still succeeded in making a name for himself as an orator in the 90s. He was drawn by his father-in-law, L. Memmius, into the circle associated with M. Livius Drusus, the tribune of 91 B.C. Following the collapse of Drusus' schemes the outbreak of the war with the Italian allies provided his opponents with an opportunity to break the careers of those who had openly supported Drusus. On the motion of the tribune Q. Varius, a court was established to prosecute those who, so it was alleged, had incited the Italians to revolt. Curio himself was a tribune in 90 B.C.; but following the prosecution of Memmius he became so afraid of public reaction that he gave up speaking in public. Then, anticipating prosecution in his turn, he fled from Italy. A promising career now lay in ruins. When we next hear of him, he is found serving with distinction with Sulla in the East. He returned to Italy with Sulla, benefited from the proscriptions, renewed his public career and reaped his reward with the consulship of 76 B.C., to be followed by a triumph and a long period of influence in the affairs of the Republic. (7) How much of this would have been possible without Sulla? The career of C. Aurelius Cotta, a near contemporary of Curio, followed much the same pattern; a good start as an orator, association with Drusus, prosecution in the quaestio Variana, flight, return with Sulla, a belated consulship in 75 B.C., then only death prevented the celebration of a triumph. (8)

It was no easy task to steer a safe course through the years 89–87 B.C. The purge by Cinna and Marius of some fourteen notable senators, including six ex-consuls, was a novel and frightening lesson in the dangers of keeping too high a profile in such times. Those opponents who evaded arrest and the relatives of the victims had little choice but to flee the country. After the killing of his brother and the suicide of his father M. Licinius Crassus went into hiding and escaped to Spain. Q. Caecilius Metellus Pius, who had come to the defence of the city against Marius and Cinna, continued resistance for some years in a new base in North Africa. Pompey found life uncomfortable in the camp of Cinna and retired to his family estates. Q. Lutatius Catulus, son of another notable victim, had already begun his own senatorial

career. Whether or not he was with Sulla in Greece, he is likely
to have left Rome. The great orator M. Antonius also lost his life
in the purge. Of his two sons who later had public careers, C.
Antonius Hibrida is known to have served as a prefect under Sulla;
he was to reach the consulship in 63 B.C. by a somewhat tortuous
route, evading conviction in the courts by dubious machinations,
but suffering expulsion from the senate in 70 B.C. because of his
debts. There were others who could tell similar stories to these.
(9)

Then there were the men whose careers were directly linked
to Sulla's success, his loyal officers, such as L. Licinius
Lucullus (cos. 74 B.C.), his brother M. Terentius Varro Lucullus,
and L. Manlius Torquatus. L. Licinius Murena (cos. 62 B.C.) began
his career as a prefect, serving alongside his father who was one
of Sulla's most capable commanders. The son achieved the
consulship which for some reason had eluded his father. A.
Gabinius (cos. 58 B.C.) may also have been the son of a Sullan
legate. Men like these owed their success directly to Sulla. (10)

Even those who stayed in Rome in the mid 80s did not
necessarily support the regime in power there, nor were they to be
classified as Sulla's opponents. No one would be likely to leave
unless he had to. For a few the chance to hold high office
beckoned. Yet even they were careful to distance themselves from
those in control and in most cases joined the winning side at an
opportune moment. L. Marcius Philippus, consul in 91 B.C. could
not resist the opportunity of the censorship in 86 B.C.; yet he was
to join Sulla and live on to be a considerable influence. His
fellow censor, M. Perperna, survived until 49 B.C. despite the
actions of his son, who continued resistance in the 70s with
Lepidus and then Sertorius. M. Pupius Piso (cos. 61 B.C.) was
quaestor in 83 B.C., but chose that moment to change sides; his
slow political advancement thereafter may owe as much to his
abrasive character as to any suspicions about his early loyalties.
Cicero himself was in Italy during this period and in his defence
of Roscius of Ameria in 80 B.C. he took the opportunity to offer an
eloquent justification of the behaviour of men like himself who had
sought throughout the reconciliation of the parties, but when that
proved impossible had joined the winning side. It was inevitable
that when a very similar situation arose in 49 B.C., Cicero looked
to the actions of men in the 80s to find a possible model for
behaviour. When he was wondering whether to remain in Italy and
come to terms with Caesar, he thought of how Philippus and others
under Cinna 'had temporized when necessary, but had taken their
opportunites when they came'. (11)

In truth Sulla's was the causa nobilitatis (the cause of
the nobility). The men who flocked to join him on his return to
Italy were not bound together by any particular creed or political
outlook. The only thing which they had in common was that their

careers were at a standstill. Sulla offered them new hope of office. What they required from him was the restoration of a res publica in which they would be the principes. This was precisely what Sulla gave them in his settlement. He recreated a political arena for them and laid down the ground rules for their orderly return to public office. Seen in this light Sulla's resignation from the dictatorship is no puzzle. It was assumed from the start to be a temporary post to restore order and to introduce the settlement. Once the cursus honorum had been restored, the men who reached the top would not tolerate the continued existence of someone with exceptional powers who might limit their libertas.

Julius Caesar is supposed to have accused Sulla of political illiteracy. (12) There is a delicious irony here. Both Sulla and Caesar used military force to take over the Roman state. Sulla used his success to make an elaborate constitutional settlement which established the rules for the public careers of the next generation; he then laid aside his powers voluntarily and died in his bed. Caesar, on the other hand, revelled in his new-found power, showed no inclination to give it up, indeed adorned it with a quasi-monarchical and religious aura unexampled in the Roman tradition, and died violently at the hands of men of whom he would have numbered many among his friends. What Sulla realised, but Caesar did not, was that the men who joined him did so not for his benefit but for their own.

If you seek to understand the men who reached the top in the last decades of the Republic, ask what they and their families were doing in the 80s. The decade had a profound effect on their attitudes. The political system which Sulla created for them was not the Republic but their Republic. It was a state in which they would be the leaders, they would reap the rewards. This explains why the sons of those who had been proscribed by Sulla were excluded from public life until the tribune M. Antonius introduced a bill on Julius Caesar's initiative. Cicero's opposition to an earlier attempt to relax the restrictions in 63 B.C. was based specifically on the need to protect the Sullan settlement from disruption. (13) Some of those who were deprived of the chance of a public career chose resistance. They joined first Lepidus in 78 B.C., then Sertorius in Spain. Cinna's son did just this. He and others like him were allowed home and were permitted to keep their citizenship under the bill of a tribune Plautius in 70 B.C. His brother-in-law, Julius Caesar, pleaded Cinna's case. But there was no hope of a public career. Only much later, in 44 B.C., did he reach the praetorship. (14) There were probably many other similar cases.

Plutarch (Caesar 6) describes Rome in the 60s as divided between two parties, the victorious one of Sulla and the beaten Marians. Although Plutarch uses language more appropriate to the politics of a Greek city state and thus is never a reliable guide to the realities of Roman republican politics, on this occasion he has a point. The term 'party' or 'faction' is inappropriate; but there were many men who had lost out in various ways because of Sulla's victory. Their fears and resentments could be exploited by politicians. So in 65 and 64 B.C. Caesar restored the public statues of Marius despite opposition from the nobility, proposed the reinstatement of the sons of the proscribed and pursued in the courts those who had carried out the most notorious killings during the proscriptions. At much the same time the younger Cato hounded those who had received rewards from Sulla during the proscriptions. Cicero, with the opportunism characteristic of a lawyer, exploited popular resentment against those who had got land and wealth from Sulla in his attacks on Rullus' land bill and on Catiline in 63 B.C. (15)

The most long-lasting effect of the troubles of the 80s was to induce in men a desperate desire to avoid a similar crisis. This caused a considerable and surprising willingness for compromise. Thus the significant modifications to Sulla's arrangements, such as the reintroduction of the state-subsidized corn supply, the restoration of the rights of tribunes and the changes to the juries, were all proposed and supported by men from the very heart of the Sullan aristocracy. Their avowed aim was to defuse potential sources of resentment in order to preserve what they considered the essentials of the system. Replying to criticism of Pompey's support for the restoration of tribunician rights, Cicero argued the case for political realism:

> When you say that you do not greatly approve of Pompey in this one matter, in my opinion you have given insufficient attention to the fact that Pompey had to consider not merely what was ideal, but what was practically necessary. For he felt that the power of a tribune was not something which could be dispensed with in our state. When originally our people had so eagerly demanded it even before they had any experience of it, how could they do without it once they had discovered its potential? Therefore the right course of action for a wise citizen was to avoid the disastrous consequences of leaving the defence of this cause to some citizen who was out to win popularity for himself, particularly when in this case what was being demanded was not in itself disastrous for the state and, indeed, was so strongly supported by the people that it would have been impossible to prevent its success. (16)

This spirit of compromise lies behind Cicero's advocacy of concordia ordinum (concord of the orders), which was less a policy, more just wishful thinking. It also explains why he and others were so reluctant to make a stand against Pompey, Crassus, and Caesar in 59 B.C. and why for so long a majority of the senate sought some solution other than war for the problem of Caesar in 50 B.C. The horrors of the 80s still had a grip on the minds of the last generation of the Republic.

3. The world of politics in the Late Republic

The testimony of Cicero makes the politics of the Late Republic by far the best documented of any period of classical history. However, for some scholars its usefulness is vitiated because in their view the period is untypical of the Republic as a whole. Such despair is premature. The aims of Roman aristocrats remained as they always had been. Sulla's settlement worked. Concentration on the peculiarities of Pompey's early career is misleading. For others regularity and certainty were restored to the pattern of public life in Rome. Nevertheless there were some new conditions which any rising politician had to take into account in planning his career.

The citizenship laws which followed the Social War opened the way for a vast new electorate to enter the assemblies. Indeed, it may well have been fear of the potential disruption to the voting assemblies which had prompted much of the opposition to wholesale grants of citizenship. The old citizens' prejudices and fears could be played upon. 'If you give citizenship to the Latins,' fulminated the consul of 122 B.C., Gaius Fannius, 'I suppose that you think that you will continue as now to find somewhere to stand to listen to a public address and attend games and public festivals? Surely you realise that they will occupy all the spaces?' Even after the settlement various devices were tried to restrict the new citizens to a small number of tribes or to keep them off the voting lists of the centuriate assembly. (17)

It may be anticipated that the Roman assemblies were potentially more volatile than earlier. From time to time the occasional tribune sought changes in the assemblies which might bring political advantage. So Sulpicius in 88 B.C. and Manilius in 66 B.C. proposed that freedmen should be allowed to cast their votes in the tribes of their ex-masters, rather than be confined to one of the four urban tribes. The radical proposal of Gaius Gracchus to mix up the order in which the centuries voted was occasionally revived without success. Clearly the proposers hoped to use their popularity to exploit the new situation which would have been created in the assemblies. (18)

The underlying assumption in all this is that the assemblies mattered. Some modern commentators tend to visualise the assemblies simply as great blocks of clients who voted at the behest of a tiny number of aristocratic patrons with the outcome predictable from the start. Although we have very little indication of the numbers who voted at elections, it is likely to have been in the tens of thousands. There is no way that the patronage system could control such numbers. In his brilliant introduction to his _Histories_ Tacitus offers a description of reactions to the death of Nero which is an acute analysis of Roman society. At the heart were the senators who were delighted at Nero's suicide. Surrounding them were the prominent members of the _equites_, the knights, who shared the senators' pleasure. In the next circle of society was the uncorrupted (_integra_) part of the people which is defined as those who are connected with great houses, their clients and freedmen. The only people who regretted the passing of Nero were the great unwashed, the _plebs sordida_, who lay outside the normal network of patronage. (19)

This last group was a far larger proportion of the population than is often allowed for. There can be little doubt that it was the floating voter who decided elections and whose support had to be won. (20) As Cicero commented,

> the people do not always give deliberate judgments in the _comitia_. They are often motivated by favouritism (_gratia_) and swayed by appeals to them (_preces_). The people elect those who solicit its votes most assiduously (_a quibus est maxime ambitus_). Even if after all it does give a deliberate judgment, it is led to that judgment not by discrimination or wisdom, but frequently by impulse and sometimes even by wild rashness.

When it suits his purpose Cicero can produce lists of eminent men who for one reason or another were unexpectedly defeated by men of lesser notability, as for example the defeat in the consular elections of 93 B.C. of L. Marcius Philippus by M. Herennius. In short 'nothing is less definite than the crowd, nothing more obscure than men's wishes, nothing more likely to confound expectations than the entire electoral system.' (21)

For those of his contemporaries (and modern scholars) who believed that _nobilitas_ was a sufficient condition for election, Cicero has a salutary lesson. When M. Juventius Laterensis, a _nobilis_, was defeated in the elections for curule aedile in 55 B.C. by a first generation senator, Cn. Plancius, he naturally assumed that the only reason could have been Plancius' use of bribery and corruption. In his defence of Plancius Cicero conceded that Juventius could expect to have had the support of all those who were dazzled by great names and by lines of ancestral busts (_imagines_); 'but if those who love _nobilitas_ are not as numerous as you supposed, how can this be our fault?' (22) Special pleading, certainly, but he had a point. Men like the Caecilii Metelli or the Domitii Ahenobarbi who were 'designated consuls in their cradles' were rarities, not the norm. In the late Republic, as at every other time, election to high office had to be worked for even by those who started with the greatest natural advantages. Sulla increased considerably the membership of the Senate. From the time of his reform there were to be 20 quaestors a year who would gain Senate membership ex officio. Although there were to be eight praetorships, instead of six, the overall result must have been to promote increased competition for the higher posts. Some of the domi nobiles, the gentry from the Italian towns, after the grant of citizenship had hopes of a senatorial career. So the pool from which magistrates might be chosen was a little enlarged. (23)

Fiercer competition for office and an enlarged potential electorate probably do much to explain the prevalence of increasingly ingenious techniques for winning an unfair advantage in elections, which a whole series of laws on ambitus did little to curb. (24)

At any time the rising politician has to take account of and pander to the sensitivities and interests of the many and varied groups within his society. In the Late Republic the equites, the Roman knights, were gradually gaining a sense of identity. This development was not to be completed until the early Principate. There is a danger in ascribing a unity of purpose and outlook to all those who used the title of eques. In the last century B.C. the term had become a generic one and covered a variety of interest groups. The eighteen centuries of the equites equo publico (knights who possess the public horse) had become an élite aristocratic status group. After 129 B.C., a man had to give up his public horse on entry into the Senate. Too much should not be made of this. There is no reason to suppose that the eighteen centuries contained men who differed significantly in background and outlook from senators. Indeed, the most easily identifiable members of the eighteen centuries were probably the sons of aristocratic, senatorial families at the early stages of their public life. Hence it was possible to identify members of the eighteen centuries as iuventus or adulescentes (young men).

The membership of the eighteen centuries was restricted; but beyond them must have been at all times many homines equestri censu ('men with the census of an eques' - 400,000 sesterces in the Late Republic), men who would have qualified for a place in the centuries if there had been places for them. Some of them were given a sense of identity when Gaius Gracchus gave them control of the juries. From then on they sought to defend their new-found privileges. The intermittent arguments about the staffing of the juries, although dressed up as disputes about equity and justice, were in reality quarrels about status. Senators resented being judged by men who were not their peers. Equites jealously guarded the right to sit on the juries because it gave them a special position in society. A third group who could be addressed as equites were the publicani, those who bid for the state contracts.

They undoubtedly included both members of the eighteen centuries and _equites_ in the broader sense. They formed a coherent and powerful pressure group who expected from magistrates the creation of the settled conditions in Rome and throughout the Roman world in which money-business could thrive. Cicero was able to boast, 'I have been concerned for the greater part of my life in cases connected with the _publicani_ and now pay eager regard to the interests of that _ordo_'. Cn. Plancius could go one better than this; his father had been a leading member of a company of _publicani_. One of the advantages which Cicero gained from his speech on the Manilian law was the opportunity to stress the importance of and his attachment to the _publicani_. Later he could claim that his suppression of the Catiline conspiracy restored confidence to a beleaguered money-market. (25)

4. The winning of support

The objectives for a Roman in public life in the Late Republic were no different from what they always had been - to win high office and a preeminent position in society. When he was elected to the consulship Cicero took the first possible opportunity to thank the people. His words reveal the same desire to be first and unique to which Q. Metellus' funeral laudation (see p.3 above) was eloquent testimony a century and a half earlier.

> I am the first 'new man' after a very long time,
> almost more remote than any contemporary can
> remember, whom you have made consul.... You not
> only elected me consul, which in itself is a very
> high honour, but you did so in a way in which few
> nobles in this state have been made consuls and no
> 'new men' before me.... I am the only one of all
> the 'new men' that we can remember who became a
> candidate for the consulship at the first
> opportunity permitted by law and won it on the
> first occasion on which I campaigned for it. (26)

Three years earlier Cicero had reached the praetorship of 66 B.C. It was undoubtedly with an eye to his campaign for the consulship that he chose this moment to appear before the people at a _contio_ (public meeting) to support the proposal of the tribune, Manilius, to give the command against Mithridates to Pompey. Cicero began his speech with what at first seems to be a somewhat surprising statement that although an appearance before the people offered unrivalled opportunities to an orator, the plan which he had made at the beginning of his career had not allowed him to make such a speech before this occasion. Cicero was saying that he had been able to rise to the praetorship without ever making a public political statement. Furthermore, when he does lend his support to a political issue, it represented a fine piece of calculated self-interest rather than a stand on a matter of principle. He had

to weigh the disadvantages of being associated with a tribune like
Manilius with the great potential gain of Pompey's support and
gratitude. Once he had made the gesture the nobility had to be
reassured that 'if we seemed to have spoken in the manner of a
popularis, we did so with a view to attracting Cn. Pompeius to our
side, so that we might have that highly influential man either as a
friend (amicus) in our campaign or at least not actively opposed to
us'. It is assumed that this argument would be understood and
accepted. (27)

If, then, Cicero had not risen up the cursus honorum as
the representative of a political viewpoint, how had he done it?
In his speech on the Manilian law he ascribed his success in the
praetorian elections to his success in the law courts. In a vivid
passage in his defence of M. Aemilius Scaurus, Cicero remarked, 'On
every hand I find matter for my use in the defence of M. Scaurus,
wherever not just my mind but even my eyes turn. The Senate house
over there bears witness to the most weighty and brave leadership
of his father.' The temple of Castor and Pollux, the temples on
the Capitol and the temple of Vesta were all pointed out by Cicero
as witnesses to the achievements of his client's forebears. (28)
In this exposition Cicero was exploiting a fact which it is easy to
forget. The public courts were held at Rome in the open air at
various points in the Forum. Wooden, later stone, tribunals were
established for the praetors' chairs. On occasion the Forum could
be full of courts. In the mid-70s B.C. one of the tribunals near
the temple of Castor was provided with steps for spectators. (29)
Trials could attract large crowds: 'I spoke in defence of Bestia
on a charge of electoral corruption before the tribunal of the
praetor Cn. Domitius in the middle of the Forum and in the presence
of a very great crowd'. (30) So even without engaging in politics
Cicero and others could become widely known and recognized. The
aim was to become 'a good man whom the whole Forum and every
tribunal sees'. (31) Indeed, in 59 B.C., when Cicero saw no role
for himself in politics, he turned back to the courts, knowing full
well that he could in this way still keep himself in the public
eye: 'My present manner of life is such as daily to increase my
popularity and resources. I keep absolutely clear of politics and
devote myself industriously to my cases and forensic work, which I
perceive is a fine road to the favour not only of those who use my
services but of the general public (vulgus) as well.' (32)

It is necessary to be precise about the causal connection
which Cicero saw between his activities in the courts and his
electoral success. As will be suggested below, the main role of
the senator was taken to be not just as an adviser on the great
matters of state but also as a 'broker', a man who used his
position, office and influence in society to solve problems, right
wrongs and obtain privileges for those who requested his help.
'Your election campaign is founded to a very large degree upon the
sort of amici (friends) you have won as a result of your

appearances for the defence in court.' Those whom he had defended were put under an obligation to support him and brought with them their friends and associates: 'Within the last two years you have laid under obligation to yourself four collegia (guilds), those of C. Fundanius, Q. Gallius, C. Cornelius and C. Orchivius, all men who have great influence in electioneering. In entrusting their case to you I know what the members of their collegia undertook and promised to you.' (33)

Again, Cicero's activities in court won him the support of men in the local communities of Italy who could play an important part in elections. His defence of men like Roscius of Ameria, Varenus of Fulginiae, Scamander of Aletrium (near Arpinum) and Cluentius of Larinum could not but help bring him advantages. In his defence of Cluentius, Cicero noted the presence in court of a large number of local aristocrats who had come to watch and support Cluentius. Cicero's speeches on behalf of the lady from Arretium and later Caecina of Volaterrae created a connection which was to last for much of his lifetime during which he consistently looked after the interests of these communities when they were affected by decisions made at Rome. Finally Cicero displayed the fact that his rhetorical abilities were at the disposal of all sorts and conditions of men, such as D. Matrinius, a scriba. (34)

'There are two skills which can raise men to the highest level of dignitas: one is that of a general, the second that of a good orator.' The alternative to a career in the courts was the army. In some ways the latter was preferable because, as Cicero pointed out, in many cases it was 'generals, not interpreters of phrases, who are chosen at consular elections'. Service in the army brought Cn. Plancius into contact with some notable and influential aristocratic generals. Murena won a great reputation as a legate with Lucullus in the East. His election campaign for the consulship was significantly advantaged by the presence of men from those campaigns who had come to Rome to take part in Lucullus' triumph. (35)

Beyond those who could be put under a specific obligation to vote for a candidate, it was essential also to win a wider popularity. At the very least, as Quintus in the Commentariolum rather cynically but realistically noted, the term amicus (friend) has to have a wider meaning in an election campaign than in the rest of life. Anyone who shows any sympathy towards you, who cultivates you, who comes frequently to your house can be labelled 'friend'. The best, though expensive, way to win popularity was to put on games and make gifts to be distributed to the members of your tribe. (36)

The Roman aristocrat was a one-man band. In order to be elected to high office, he had to put together an elaborate, but entirely temporary, coalition of interest-groups and individuals who would anticipate favours and rewards from the successful candidate. The consulship was a post with <u>imperium</u> (the recognised right to give orders to others) which gave the holder not only considerable control of the major affairs of state, but also unparalleled opportunities for winning glory for himself and for dispensing favours and rewards to others. These factors help to create the 'bandwagon' effect which is familiar to any student of American presidential campaigns. While the outcome of the race is uncertain, people will support their initial favourites; but when a potential winner emerges, then voters will race to join him. Failure to be able to demonstrate support for one of the victors meant exclusion from access to those with power and influence for the next year.

In July 65 B.C. P. Sulpicius Galba, a man of unstained character but lacking in energy, began his campaign for election as consul for 63 B.C. well before anyone else. The results were disastrous for him, because he failed to get strong declared support. Cicero was pleased because those canvassed by Galba claimed that their obligations bound them to Cicero in the first instance. Cicero hoped that his campaign would really get rolling when it became widely known that he had so many friends. (37) When Cn. Plancius stood for the aedileship, his campaign received the open support of the numerous distinguished local gentry of his own community. They lent his campaign dignity (<u>dignitas</u>), ensured that all eyes were turned on Plancius and were constant, unwavering and persistent in their attendance upon him. This did much to win over the support of the gentlemen from neighbouring communities. (38)

So it was essential for a candidate to look a winner. 'See that your campaign is full of show (<u>pompa</u>)', advises the <u>Commentariolum</u>. It was important to be seen to be popular. Upon waking, the candidate would expect to find his house thronged with well-wishers at the <u>salutatio</u> (morning greeting). Such men were making a minimal, but nonetheless important, contribution to the campaign. They might attend the <u>salutationes</u> of more than one candidate and in any case their duty was soon performed and they could go about their business. More important were those who were prepared to give up the time to accompany the candidate from his house down to the Forum each day (the <u>deductio</u>). A good crowd contributed to the <u>opinio</u> and <u>dignitas</u> of the candidate. Finally there were those who were prepared to devote all their energies to constant attendance on the candidate (<u>adsectatio</u>). It was essential at all times to be surrounded by a crowd (<u>cum multitudine esse</u>), to give the impression that such men gathered because of the favours which the candidate could dispense. It was inevitable that envious opponents would seek to show that in fact it was money rather than friendship which brought these crowds together – a practice which went against the various laws on electoral corruption. (39)

In ways such as these the candidate sought to build for himself the image of a winner so as to extend his influence beyond those who were under a specific obligation to him to the uncommitted voter who was so vital at any election. The aim was a creation of an ad hoc, loose-knit coalition of interests of the sort which Cicero describes in a letter of 53 B.C. about the campaign of Milo for the consulship:

> We have much on our side: the support of the respectable men (bonorum studium); the favour of the crowd and the common people (vulgi ac multitudinis) which was gained by the magnificence of Milo's games and his natural liberality; the support of the young men (iuventutis) and the men of influence in elections because of his out-standing support (gratia) and diligence towards this kind of person. (40)

5.   Aggressive individualism

In the modern democratic state we are used to politics having the appearance of being an adversarial debate between party members who represent constituencies. Little or nothing of this applies to politics in the Roman world. The Roman aristocrat saw his life differently. Cicero has the Elder Cato remark that even in old age 'the Senate (curia) is not deprived of his abilities, nor are the rostra, nor his friends (amici), clients or guest-friends (hospites)'. It would be wrong to suppose that the Senate-house was the centre of his existence. Any aristocrat could normally expect to hold office only for a very few years of his life. Membership of the Senate was for life; but the range of major issues to be decided there was limited. More of his time would be spent in the defence of amici in the courts. This last activity is one aspect of the real day-to-day role of the senator as a broker, an intermediary who at the request of an individual, group or community used his influence to obtain favours and get things done. (41)

Book XIII of Cicero's Letters to Friends is the key. Here are collected a selection of Cicero's 'letters of commendation' (litterae commendaticiae). Most of them come from just two years in Cicero's career; but letters such as these must have formed the bulk of Cicero's correspondence throughout his career. They tend to take a standard form. Someone approaches Cicero, a man of auctoritas and gratia, with a plea for assistance. Cicero writes to the relevant official, frequently a provincial governor, who has the power to deal with the problem, and draws his attention to the matter, while at the same time emphasizing the close bonds (necessitudo) and good will (benevolentia) which exist between the official and Cicero. Some letters were little more than testimonials which recommend a friend of Cicero for a post. Many others concern <u>negotia</u> (money-business, loans and the like) and request the official to help to secure the payment of a debt or interest on a loan. Cicero could act as the spokesman for an interest-group, such as the company of <u>publicani</u> concerned with Bithynia. He also sought to defend the interests of communities with whom he had close ties, as when the people of Volaterrae approached him to intercede with Q. Valerius Orca, one of the commissioners in charge of the land allotments for Caesar's veterans. More exotically, the community of Sparta chose Cicero to represent their interests to the current governor of Achaea. Of such stuff were the day-to-day politics of Rome made. The historian who does not divert his attention from the great issues of state cannot but get a distorted view of the realities of the Roman Republic. (42)

The Roman aristocrat was an aggressive individual. Roman public life forced him to compete rather than cooperate. After Sulla twenty men were elected to the quaestorship every year. For a few of them this was the height of their ambition, but most would hope that this was only the beginning of their rise to the consulship. However, there were only two consulships each year and so nearly all of those who set out as quaestors would have to fail at some point on the climb up the pyramid of power. Therefore the ambitious young aristocrat had to look on most of his contemporaries as potential rivals. Such a system was unlikely to produce stable political groupings. Parties, factions and family groups in Roman politics are largely the creation of modern commentators. The ancient historian constantly seeks ways of filling the huge gaps in the evidence. Therefore, if a Roman politician could be identified with a policy or located in a political group, it would be possible to infer from his known actions to his likely position on issues for which the evidence of his attitude is lacking. Unfortunately no such stable groups existed. The coalition of interests which each politician had to put together to get elected was complex, transitory and entirely personal to that individual.

The language of <u>partes</u> ('parties'), and <u>factio</u> ('faction') was largely the language of partisan rhetoric rather than of objective and precise historical description. It made no sense to ask of a Roman aristocrat in normal times to which party he belonged. 'Partes' could be said to exist only at times of crisis, when people were forced to take sides. So Cicero can state with disapproval that the death of Tiberius Gracchus and his conduct beforehand of his entire tribunate had divided a united people into two <u>partes</u>. The people of Massilia in 49 B.C. 'recognised that the Roman people had split into two parties... and that the leaders of these two parties were Gnaeus Pompey and Gaius Caesar'. At such times of crisis this partisanship could have an effect on elections. In 50 B.C., a vacancy occurred in the college of Augurs upon the death of Q. Hortensius. The two candidates were M.

Antonius, who had only held the quaestorship but was an open supporter of Julius Caesar, and L. Domitius Ahenobarbus, the distinguished consul of 54 B.C., who was a vociferous opponent of Caesar throughout the 50s. Ahenobarbus was defeated in an election in which 'people's support was displayed in accordance with party feelings and only a very few were moved by personal loyalty (<u>necessitudo</u>) to show their support'. (43)

If the Roman aristocrat would not in normal times claim to belong to any party, he would be insulted at the notion that he was a member of a <u>factio</u>. This term is a word of abuse used to describe one's enemies who had banded together in an abnormal way with the aim of controlling the political system. What constituted a <u>factio</u> depended on your point of view. Catiline and his followers may be abused as constituting a <u>factio</u>; on the other hand, according to Sallust, Catiline claimed that he left Rome to escape the <u>factio</u> of his enemies. The coalition of Pompey, Crassus and Caesar in 59 B.C. might be seen as a <u>factio</u> by those outside it; but in 49 B.C. Caesar could claim that his invasion of Italy was to free the Roman people from the oppression of a <u>factio</u> of a minority. (44)

There were no parties; but what about policies? Once again it is easy to be misled by images taken from modern representative democracy. The Roman aristocrat represented no one but himself. He had no constituency. His commitment to causes was purely temporary in so far as they promoted his own aggrandisement. Occasionally issues could dominate an election. Gaius Marius in his campaign for the consulship of 107 B.C. was able to exploit widespread resentment about the conduct of the war with Jugurtha. (45) Much more often the candidate could not afford to take a stand on an issue for fear of alienating some support. In his election campaign he had to be all things to all men. (46) Further there were comparatively few matters for which a senator had to form a policy at any time. It is a characteristic of governments in modern states that they intervene significantly in a great many aspects of their citizens' lives. Not so in Rome. Citizens were not taxed; there was little in the way of 'social services' to be decided upon. Such great matters as there were, war, peace and treaties, were decided at least formally by the Senate and People of Rome; but both the detailed conduct and, indeed, often the broad aspects of policy lay in the hands of the annual magistrates with <u>imperium</u>. Whether the Senate was permitted to discuss the matter at all could depend on the wish of the presiding magistrate. Significantly, on 8 November 63 B.C. Cicero as consul refused to permit a senatorial debate on the evidence to back up his case against Catiline. (47)

Surprisingly, perhaps, the evidence rarely allows us a detailed account of senatorial proceedings. What evidence there is does not suggest a high level debate. In the mid-50s B.C. Ptolemy

Auletes, the nominal king of Egypt, sought desperately to get Roman backing for his restoration to his throne from which he had been driven by his irate subjects. In a series of letters from January 56 Cicero keeps P. Cornelius Lentulus, the governor of Cilicia and an interested party, informed of the discussions in the Senate. The whole sorry affair seems to contain little or no discussion of policy or of the rights and wrongs of the case. Candidates for the prestigious job vied with each other to promote their own cause and impede their rivals. (48)

Concentration on the squabbles which arose from time to time between individuals or groups in the Republic should not be allowed to hide the fundamental unity of outlook of Rome's ruling class. Modern scholars who have in mind the model of politics which are carried on by adversaries who represent radically different viewpoints have sought to find a parallel in Republican politics. They have often found it in Cicero's description of the two types of men in the Roman state, optimates and populares. However, once again it is important to realise that this is a piece of courtroom advocacy, not political analysis. (49)

In Cicero's formulation optimates were those who accepted the status quo and were ready to defend religious observance, the power and authority of the magistrates and the Senate, the laws, ancestral custom, the judicial system, credit, the empire, the army and the state treasury. That these are not a precise or close-knit group in the state is shown by the fact that Cicero suggests that anyone from leading politicians, senators, local gentry, men engaged in negotia, even freedmen could be optimates. This is surely Cicero's concordia ordinum ('concord of the orders') under another guise. It is a piece of wishful thinking which amounted to little more than a belief that if all good men and true could agree then problems would simply vanish.

In this passage populares are hardly defined at all, simply abused as criminals and revolutionaries. In fact the characteristic of a popularis was a method of political action which was open to any ambitious politician. To act populariter ('in a popular manner') was to be ready to present straight to the popular assemblies bills which were designed to deal with the problems of ordinary people, including land, the supply of corn and the persistent problem of debt. Such bills displayed a willingness to use all the resources of the state to solve the problems; so it was a typical criticism of populares that their proposals 'exhausted the treasury'. (50) Some of the men who used these methods may have been disinterested reformers; but it was always assumed that their primary motive was the winning of widespread popular support for election to high office. Thus the opposition to M. Livius Drusus, the popular tribune of 91 B.C., was motivated by the fear that by his bill granting citizenship to the Italians he might gain such great support that he could wield tyrannical power in the state. (51) In his opposition to Rullus' land bill of 63 B.C., one of the most enlightened proposals of the Late Republic, Cicero curdles the blood of his contemporaries by representing the colonies which Rullus proposed to establish in Italy as garrisons of men ready to march at Rullus' bidding. (52) This was a total distortion; but fellow aristocrats, particularly those who were engaged in the same political race as the popularis tribune, were unlikely to support a measure which would have greatly increased the popular support of the proposer and have given him a distinct advantage in future elections. Popularis techniques were open to any aspiring politician to use, particularly in the early stages of his career. The widespread popular support gained by such methods, when tribune, would stand a man in good stead when he became a candidate for higher office, even if he would then seek to play down his earlier tactics.

6. The end of the Republic

Aristocrats who used popularis techniques were in no sense 'left wing radicals' who sought to change the political system. Indeed, they would claim that they belonged to a perfectly respectable political tradition which was designed to maintain the Republican system by defusing areas of tension which threatened stability and concord. When Livy came to write his history of the Republic, he reflected this tradition. His accounts of early corn-doles and land grants are full of words like blandimenta, dulcedo, indulgentia. He saw them as acts designed to reconcile the ordinary people to the political status quo. So, commenting on an early corn dole and other measures, Livy notes that 'this act of indulgence by the Senators kept the state harmonious' (concordia). (53) However, in the Late Republic the Senate and consuls initiated hardly any major pieces of social legislation. The significant reforms came from tribunes, often in the face of fierce opposition from other senators. Many failed even to recognise the existence of the problems. Consider Cicero's speeches against Rullus' land bill. There is not the slightest acknowledgement that there is a problem to be solved, not one word of sympathy for the poor and the landless. (54)

It would be wrong simply to castigate Cicero and his colleagues for blind selfishness. In their view people's problems could be solved by the exercise of private patronage, the intervention of the state was unnecessary and undesirable. The trouble was that the help which could be given by an individual was limited. Cicero's de officiis ('On Duties') is illuminating on all aspects of the aristocrat's use of property. Liberalitas is good, indeed essential. But the act must do no harm to anyone else; it must not be beyond one's means; and it must be in proportion to the worthiness of the recipient (compare the Victorian notion of the 'deserving poor'). (55) Unfortunately in the Late Republic the scale of the problems of land, debt and the food supply were too great to be solved by these means. Increasing numbers of people did not have access to the charmed circles of private patronage. Curiously Cicero chanced in the same work to notice the inevitable outcome of such a situation: 'When the poverty-stricken masses were oppressed by those who had greater wealth, they fled for protection to some one man who was conspicuous for his virtue. He shielded those who were less well-off from wrong.' (56)

The political squabbles and the race for preeminence in the Late Republic thwarted what efforts there were to deal with the problems of the ordinary citizen. It was only after 49 B.C. that in the name of Julius Caesar there was enacted a significant body of social legislation to deal with debt and land-settlement. Augustus in this as in so much else was to learn from and improve upon his adopted father's efforts. The age of the 'super-patron' had arrived.

Notes

1. Cicero _ad Att._ IX 10.3 (18 March 49 B.C.).

2. Cicero _ad Att._ VII 1.4 (16 October 50 B.C.).

3. See for example: Cicero _ad Att._ VII 7.7; VIII 3.6, 11.2; IX 7.3, 7c. 1, 10.3 and 6, 14.2, 15.2; X 7.1, 8.7.

4. If it came to war then Cicero was not in doubt: 'better to be defeated with the one (Pompey), rather than be victorious with the other (Caesar)' (_ad Att._ VII 1.4). For Cicero's hope of a triumph: _ad fam._ XV 4, 5, 6, 10, 13; _ad Att._ VI 3.3, 6.4, 8.5, 9.2; VII 4.2, 7.4, on which see M.Wistrand, _Cicero Imperator_ (Göteburg 1979).

5. Caelius: Cicero _ad fam._ VIII 14.3. On the issues in the civil war see K.Raaflaub, _Dignitatis contentio_ (Munich 1974).

6. Cicero _in Cat._ III 25.

7. C. Scribonius Curio: lack of formal education: Cicero _Brutus_ 210; his career threatened: Asconius 74C, Cicero _Brutus_ 305; service with Sulla: Plutarch _Sulla_ 14.7, Appian _Mith._ 60; return with Sulla: Cicero _Brutus_ 311, Schol. Bob. 89 St; consulship, proconsulship in Macedonia, triumph over the Dardani: Broughton _MRR_ II 92, 118.

8. C. Aurelius Cotta: early career: Cicero _Brutus_ 202; trial: Appian _B.C._ I 37; out of Rome in the 80s: _Brutus_ 227; return

with Sulla: Brutus 311; consul 75 B.C.: see Broughton MRR II
96, n.b.: description in Sallust Hist. III 48. 8M: ex factione
media consul ('a consul from the very heart of the ruling
faction', for this interpretation see R.Seager, JRS 62 (1972)
57); death on eve of triumph: Cicero in Pis. 62, Asconius 14C.

9.   The purge by Cinna and Marius: Appian B.C. I 71f. Crassus:
Cicero pro Sestio 48, Plutarch Crassus 4 ff. (the date of his
exile may have been some time after the deaths of his father
and brother, see Plutarch Crassus 6). Q. Caecilius Metellus
Pius: Plutarch Marius 42, Appian B.C. I 80. Pompey: Plutarch
Pompey 5. Q. Lutatius Catulus: Schol. Bob. 176 St, Gran. Lic.
25B; his presence on a legatio in 87 B.C. suggests that he was
already a senator. If he was already aedile (Ammianus XIV
6.25), then his career may have been held up for a few years
in the Cinnan period and he would reach his consulship in 78
B.C. a few years late, contra G.V.Sumner, The Orators in
Cicero's Brutus (Phoenix Supplementary Vol. XI, Toronto 1973)
116. A dedication in Athens may suggest his presence there
with Sulla (B. Merritt, Hesperia 1954, 254). C. Antonius,
consul 63 B.C.: father killed in purge: Appian B.C. I 72;
prefect in Greece with Sulla: Asconius 84C; later trial:
Asconius loc.cit. and Plutarch Caesar 4, Comm. Pet. 8;
expelled from Senate in 70 B.C.: Asconius 84 C. For others
one wonders, for example, what happened to L. Octavius (consul
75 B.C.), a relative of Cn. Octavius, consul 87 B.C., who was
killed by Cinna and Marius.

10.   L. Licinius Lucullus: Plutarch Lucullus. His brother (consul
73 B.C.): Plutarch Sulla 27.7, Lucullus 37. L. Manlius
Torquatus (consul 65 B.C.) was Sulla's proquaestor and was at
the battle of the Colline Gate, although the evidence of his
presence in the East with Sulla is flimsy: M.Crawford, Roman
Republican Coinage (Cambridge 1974) I 80, 386 (coins not
minted in the East, as some have suggested), Plutarch Sulla
29, Nepos Att. 1.4, Cicero Fin. I 39. Murena: Cicero pro
Murena 11. Gabinius: perhaps the son of Sulla's legate or,
indeed, he may be identified with the legate: Plutarch Sulla
16 f., App. Mith. 66 (for the identification see E. Badian,
Philologus 103 (1959) 87 ff).

11.   For the censorship of Philippus and Perperna: Broughton MRR II
54. Cicero de domo sua 84 shows clearly that Philippus was
reluctant to exclude his uncle Appius Claudius Pulcher from
the senate list; but that legally there was nothing he could
do because Claudius' imperium had been abrogated by a
tribunician bill presented to the people. Philippus' action
should not be seen as cooperation with the Cinnan regime as
E.Badian, JRS 52 (1962), 52 suggests. For Perperna's long
life: Pliny NH VII 156. M. Pupius Piso (consul 61 B.C.):
quaestor in 83 B.C., Cicero Verr. II 1.37; on his character

and career: Cicero *Brutus* 236. Cicero on the civil war: *pro Rosc. Am.* 136; Cicero on Philippus: *ad Att.* VIII 3.6.

12. Suetonius *DJ* 77 (although note that the source for the remark is an anti-Caesarian one).

13. On the children of the proscribed: Plutarch *Sulla* 31, Velleius II 28; on Cicero's opposition to restoration: *ad Att.* II 1.3, *Pis.* 4, Quintilian *Inst.* XI 1.85; on the *Lex Antonia* in 49 B.C.: Dio XLI 18.2, Suetonius *DJ* 41, Plutarch *Caesar* 37.

14. Cinna's recall: Suetonius *DJ* 5, Gellius *NA* XIII 3.5, Dio XLIV 47.4.

15. See B.A.Marshall, *Historia* 33 (1984) 199 ff. Caesar: Suetonius *DJ* 11, Velleius II 43. Cato: Plutarch *Cato* 17.4. Cicero on Sullan landholders: *de lege agraria* II 68, III passim, *in Cat.* II 20. On the exploitation of *invidia* (hostility) against Sullan landholders see W.V.Harris, *Rome in Etruria and Umbria* (Oxford 1971) 289ff.

16. Cicero *de legibus* III 26.

17. Fannius: ORF(2) p.144. On the new citizens: Appian *B.C.* I 55, Livy *Ep.* 77, cf. T.P.Wiseman, *JRS* 59 (1969) 59 ff.

18. On freedmen: Livy *Ep.* 77, Dio XXXVI 42, Asconius 52C, see S.Treggiari, *Roman Freedmen during the Late Republic* (Oxford 1969) 37 ff. C. Gracchus: (Sallust) *ad Caes.* II 8.1. On the composition of the electorate: C. Nicolet, *The World of the Citizen in Republican Rome* (London 1980) 226 ff.

19. Tacitus *Histories* I 4.

20. *Comm. Pet.* 16 divides an election campaign into two activities: the winning of *amici* (friends) and of the goodwill of the people (*popularis voluntas*).

21. Cicero *pro Plancio* 9, 12, *pro Murena* 36.

22. Cicero *pro Plancio* 18.

23. See T.P.Wiseman, *New Men in the Roman Senate 139 B.C. - A.D. 14* (Oxford 1971).

24. On legislation against *ambitus* see E. Gruen, *The Last Generation of the Roman Republic* (Berkeley 1974) 212 ff.

25. On the definition of *equites* see T.P.Wiseman, *Historia* 19 (1970) 67 ff., contra C.Nicolet, *L'Ordre Equestre* (Paris 1966). *Plebiscitum equorum reddendorum* ('bill on handing back

horses'): Cicero rep. IV 2. Equites as iuventus and adulescentuli: Comm. Pet. 33. On the equites and their interests see P.Brunt, 'The Equites in the Late Republic', reprinted in R.Seager (ed.), The Crisis of the Roman Republic (Cambridge 1969) 117 ff. Cicero as advocate of the publicani: Cicero Verr. II 2.181; Plancius: Schol. Bob. 157 St., Cicero pro Plancio 37; Cicero de lege Manilia 17, ad fam. V 6.2.

26. Cicero de lege agraria II 3.

27. Cicero de lege Manilia 1; Comm. Pet. 5.

28. Cicero pro Scauro 46 ff.

29. The forum full of courts: Cicero Verr. II 5.143; for the remains of the stone gradus Aurelii near the temple of Castor (cf. Cicero pro Flacco 66), see E.Nash, Pictorial Dictionary of Ancient Rome (London 1962) II 478 ff.

30. Cicero ad QF II 3.6, cf. Asconius 54 C: the trial of Cornelius in 65 B.C. took place before a great crowd (magno conventu); Cicero pro Archia 3.

31. Horace Ep. I 16.57.

32. Cicero ad Att. II 22.3.

33. Comm. Pet. 20 and 19.

34. For the importance of men of influence (gratiosi) in the Italian towns: Comm. Pet. 24; for Cicero's cases: pro Rosc. Am., Quintilian Inst. Or. IV 1.74, pro Cluentio, particularly 49 and 197; for Arretium and Volaterra: pro Caecina, especially 97, ad Att. I 19.4, ad fam. XIII 4 and 54; readiness to defend men of all classes: Comm. Pet. 3, pro Cluentio 126.

35. Cicero pro Murena 30, 38; pro Plancio 27; pro Murena 20, 37.

36. Comm. Pet. 16; pro Murena 38 ff.; de Off. II 56.

37. Galba: Asconius 82 C, Comm. Pet. 7, ad Att. I 1.1.

38. Cicero pro Plancio 19 ff.

39. Comm. Pet. 52, 34-7, pro Murena 70.

40. Cicero ad fam. II 6.3.

41. Cicero de sen. 32. For the division of the aristocrat's life between the Sebate and looking after friends see: Brutus 165, 245, pro Sulla 26, ad fam. IV 5.3.

42. Cicero ad fam. XIII passim; for testimonials see e.g. XIII 31, 40, 51; for negotia: XIII 43, 69, 72: for the publicani: XIII 9, cf. 65; Volaterrae: XIII 4 and 5; Sparta: XIII 28b.

43. Cicero Rep. I 31; Caesar B.C. I 35.3; Cicero ad fam. VIII 14.1.

44. On factio see R.Seager, JRS 62 (1972) 53 ff. Sallust Cat. 34.2, Caesar B.C. I 22.

45. Sallust Jug. 85 etc.

46. Comm. Pet. 5, 45 ff.

47. Cicero in Cat. I 20.

48. Cicero ad fam. I 1-7, cf. I.Shatzman, Latomus 30 (1971), 363 ff.

49. Cicero pro Sestio 96 ff.

50. e.g. Cicero pro Sestio 103, commenting of C. Gracchus' corn law.

51. (Sallust) ad Caes. II 6.3.

52. Cicero de lege agraria II 16.

53. Livy II 9.

54. Cicero absolves himself from any sense of responsibility for the plight of the poor farmers by assuming that they had got themselves into this mess by their own irresponsibility: Cat. II 20, cf. Sallust Cat. 28.

55. Cicero de off. I 42.

56. Cicero de off. II 41.

3. The Politics of the Early Principate

BARBARA LEVICK

1.   Political issues

Even in societies committed to revolutionary change (France after 1789, Russia after 1917) old features are retained, or return: children learn more from their parents than they are taught. In 'the Roman Revolution' ideals and ideology subsisted; only the techniques changed, in particular through the development of violence as a political means, and the personalities, each dynast carrying with him as he rose a swarm of followers, men who in pre-revolutionary conditions might not have thought of embarking on a career in politics.

Roman politics remained a quest for fame, power, and wealth conducted by individuals who also considered themselves responsible for maintaining or advancing the fortunes of their family. They looked for support from that family and its dependants and from ad hoc groups of political associates. Such groups might be cemented by marriage, strengthened, eroded, or broken by the wear and tear of political life, by principle or self-interest. As under the Republic, the prime goal remained the consulship, both for its own sake and for the commands abroad and influence at home to which it gave access. Politics was a game with rules and prizes long familiar; the aristocracy knew no other, and they wanted to go on playing it. It was in the interest of the Princeps that they should believe they could.

If the main concern of a Roman politician was his own success, he was nonetheless involved in running the state and taking decisions on matters of policy and principle. For the last fifty years of the Republic the overriding issue had been whether the Senate or an individual was to control the state. Now what was in question was the form that the Principate was to take. Augustus himself had to shift his position in the course of his forty-four years of supremacy, leaving his successors a legacy which (like Lenin's) was open to interpretation: 'back to Augustus' sounded well, but could mean many things. At first, between 27 and 23 B.C., he seemed to be offering a Republic directed by the Senate, as it had been in the second century B.C. before the tribunates of the Gracchi had challenged senatorial supremacy; then in 23 he seemed to be taking on the mantle of the Gracchi and showing that he was the master by demanding the overriding imperium of the military dynasts. That was his reaction to opposition from leading senators in the years 24-23 B.C.; the resistance collapsed in 19, and there was no further serious effort to abolish the Principate or to diminish its prerogatives until the senatorial debates that followed the assassination of Gaius in A.D.41. (1)

Each member of the senatorial class had to make up his mind how to behave in the face of the Principate. If he took part in politics at all (see below, pp.60-1) he had a wide range of options open to him between open opposition and obsequious collaboration. Fannius Caepio had been an opponent even before he was killed as a conspirator in 23 B.C.; over against the diehards stood such men as M. Valerius Messalla Corvinus the orator (cos. 31 B.C.), who in 2 B.C. claimed to have been mandated by Senate and people to offer Augustus the title Pater Patriae. Between came men who worked with the Princeps for the state without striking attitudes or sacrificing their integrity, men such as M. Aemilius Lepidus, the consul of A.D.6, himself judged worthy to be a potential Princeps. (2)

Newcomers may not have felt the issues so strongly. They entered the Senate only after the Principate had been established and owed a debt of gratitude for their advancement (see below, pp.54f, 56f). Blatant opportunists like Cn. Domitius Afer, the orator from Narbonensis (cos. suff. 39), can be seen in their ranks. Others may not have felt at home enough in the House to allow themselves strong views. But to some senatorial government remained the ideal it had been for Cicero. For that reason, and because they were part of it, they would defend the Senate's power and prestige as best they could. Not all had the courage of Thrasea Paetus of Patavium (cos.suff. 56), to walk out of the Senate as a sign of disapproval, or of his son-in-law Helvidius Priscus of Cluviae, praetor in 70, whose hounding of the Emperor Vespasian led to his exile and death, but they took their role as senators seriously (think of Pliny the Younger!) and their rise in the Flavian period changed the tone of public and social life. (3)

When Augustus' last sustained struggle with the Senate ended, he made it clear that he meant to have a successor in power, or successors. Here was another focal point for politics, again to be seen in two ways: as a matter of interest, of backing winners who would bring their supporters power and fortune; or as one of principle: which candidate would give the Senate a better deal.

Under Augustus the issue was not finally decided until A.D.9, and it left a legacy of ill-feeling which was to damage the next reign: Tiberius found his Senate full of men who, having backed the wrong runners, resented and feared him. Similar issues polarized the politics of the twenties, with factions centring on Germanicus's sons Nero and Drusus and on the Praetorian Prefect Sejanus, who presented himself as the champion of Tiberius' grandson Gemellus; so too in the early thirties Gemellus and Gaius Caesar had their backers, and in the reign of Claudius, in the late forties and early fifties, Britannicus and Nero. (4)

2. The Senate

After twenty years of civil war, dictatorship and triumviral rule, countless senatorial families had lost their representatives in the House, and it was crowded with the partisans of the dynasts. At more than a thousand strong it was nearly twice the size that Sulla had envisaged. It was an obstacle to a return to normal politics, the parvenus blocking the way of those who saw office as their birthright. To Octavian those who had been admitted by his partners in the Triumvirate or who had not taken his side in the campaign of Actium (he claimed more than seven hundred who had) were the most objectionable. There was a good case for a purge, but strong resistance: in 29 B.C. only 190 were removed and Octavian had to go about wearing a breastplate under his toga. Three more efforts had to be made to rid the Senate of undesirables: in 18 B.C., 11 B.C., and as late as A.D. 4, when the aim may have been to help the new successor designate, Tiberius. Not only did individuals prove tenacious: the Senate as a body resented and resisted lectiones. On the second occasion Augustus reached the Sullan level of 600 men, but it is said that he would have preferred the impossible pre-Sullan figure of 300. It was a problem that would diminish as the triumviral generation died out. Like Sulla, Augustus set the number of quaestors entering the Senate every year at twenty, but he lowered the age at which the magistracy could be held from thirty to twenty-five (or just under); the Senate should eventually have settled down at well below 600 members, probably at not more than 450-500. (5)

The stability of the Senate was guaranteed by regulations about its future intake. A property qualification was established, formally perhaps for the first time; set originally at the equestrian census of 400,000 sesterces, it had risen by 12 B.C. probably to one million. (6) Other qualifications, of birth and character, were also demanded. These rules should have freed senators from the fear of the arbitrary pronouncements of the censors; that office was never held after 22 B.C., except occasionally by Principes. Nonetheless men were weeded out from time to time, usually on the grounds of poverty (see below, p.58).

In a moving ceremony held in the House on 16 January, 27 B.C., Augustus completed what he himself called the transfer of the Republic from his power to the sway of Senate and people. Even after the Principate had been in existence for nearly sixty years, a loyal senator could describe this settlement by saying that 'validity was restored to the laws, authority to the courts, and dignity to the Senate; the power of the magistrates was reduced to its former limits.... The old traditional form of the Republic was restored.' Velleius Paterculus' use of the word 'form' is significant: it comprises the rules, written and conventional, that should govern the working of politics. (7)

Velleius also speaks of the dignity of the Senate – an important factor in the self-respect of its members. In some ways the Senate made substantial advances in power and prestige during Augustus' principate, mainly at the expense of the people's assemblies and the jury courts, which were staffed in part by equites. Legislation continued to be brought before the assemblies down to the end of the first century A.D., but it is likely to have been approved by the Senate beforehand; and the Senate could be effective in blocking or delaying legislation unwelcome to it. As the quantity of business brought before the comitia declined, senatorial decrees multiplied and became an unchallenged source of law. (8) In the judicial sphere the Senate itself was acting as a court of law by the end of Augustus' reign: a particularly vicious case of misgovernment in Asia was taken cognizance of in the House and punished by a senatus consultum ordaining exile. Tacitus regularly shows cases of adultery and high treason, as well as extortion, taken by the Senate when the accused are persons of rank. This much prized but dangerous privilege was eroded when Claudius began to try senators himself without bringing them before the House; that was one of the most disliked features of his regime. (9)

Dignity did accrue to the Senate under Augustus; but the existence of a permanent dynast combining the powers of consul and tribune, and controlling by far the greater part of the army, could not fail to detract from its real powers and independence. Lip-service might be paid to Livy's claim (written in the earliest years of the Principate) that it was the Senate's place to determine what was best for itself and the state, but the Princeps was an acknowledged originator of policy, while his imperium made him a source of law as well. Augustus had the right to bring business before it and supervised the agenda of the Senate besides. A committee of the consuls, other magistrates, and fifteen senators prepared business. What went to the full Senate with their backing must have been what the Princeps wanted. In Augustus' last year, when he was unable to attend the Senate, the recommendations of the committee were given the force of senatus consulta. Not surprisingly, Tiberius, who held minimalist views about the role of the Princeps, abolished that body. Equally unsurprisingly, it is clear that by Nero's reign the Senate was discussing largely what was remitted to it by Nero's informal consilium, and that matters that arose in the Senate itself would not proceed to a formal motion without being referred back to him. (10)

If the Senate were recalcitrant over an important matter, Augustus could resort to plain bullying, as he did in A.D. 5-6, when he was trying to introduce a means of financing pensions for retired soldiers by setting up a special treasury to be supplied by a tax on inheritances. On that occasion he invoked the late Dictator as the author of the scheme. (11) It was not often necessary to be so crude. The Senate listened attentively to the suggestions of the Princeps: each senator knew that the Princeps could control his career, sometimes decisively.

Allowance must be made for changes of source, but it is noticeable how the quality and significance of senatorial debate diminishes in the pages of Tacitus. Tiberius muttered that the senators were ready for slavery; Claudius openly rebuked them for not speaking their minds. The first years of Nero's principate were advertised as a time of revival, but impatient senators complained of the triviality of what was discussed. The last time the Senate could be seen digging its toes in was in 48, when Claudius advocated admitting Gauls to membership. It was a significant sticking point, and shows the Senate's preoccupations. (12)

If the Senate as a whole deferred to the Princeps, so much the more did individual magistrates. Abroad, his imperium was greater than theirs; at home his auctoritas put him above them all, a fact which was brought home to the aediles by Tiberius in 22, when they brought up the question of extravagance: he hinted that they might have consulted him first, and pointed out that he performed the functions neither of aediles nor of praetors nor of consuls: something grander, loftier, was expected of the Princeps. (13)

After his attempts to purge the Senate, Augustus had to be careful about admitting new men. He did not bring men of non-senatorial family into the House at a certain rank, co-opting them as tribunicii, for example, as the later imperial censors did and as Domitian's successors did without being censor. Instead, he gave cautious help to protégés as they made their way from magistracy to magistracy.

Nonetheless, men from further afield than ever before began to try their luck. Into the old bottles of the cursus honorum, as refurbished by Sulla, had already been poured a quantity of new wine: men of substance from the country towns of Italy who were now qualified for membership. Under Augustus that process was completed (the Paeligni, who had played their part in

the Social War, did not produce their first senator until the
second decade of Augustus' principate); only a favoured few came
from the provinces. It is significant that Augustus had to raise
the number of praetorships from the Sullan eight to ten, twelve,
and on one occasion late in his principate, to fifteen; the figure
of eighteen was reached in Claudius' reign, and that of Nero saw
bitter quarrels in the House over the office. (14) The praetorship
was the level that the ambitious newcomer might expect to reach;
even with twelve posts available each year, and a high death rate,
there would have been disappointed new men after each praetorian
election, for the demands of the nobility would be the first to be
met. To the consulship not all aspired, and the two suffect posts
normally offered after 5 B.C. relieved some of the pressure.

The accession of new men to the Senate in large numbers
during the twenty years before Actium and more gradually afterwards
contributed to a change in the meaning of a political term:
nobilis. (15) Under the Republic the consulship, perhaps any
curule office, ennobled a man and his descendants. It was
questionable whether office obtained in the years of revolution or
after the end of the Republic (whatever arbitrary date we fix for
that) had the same effect. At any rate, more subtle distinctions
of nobilitas began to be drawn: descent in the female line came to
count, for instance. The change from Republic to Principate thus
gave the Roman upper class an opportunity to refine still further
its sensibility to matters of rank and privilege - and so helped to
preserve the distinctions. Each rank knew what rewards it might
expect to obtain, if there was no question of extraordinary ability
or luck. Ordinarius consulships and the most prestigious
priesthoods, especially if they are awarded early in life, are
indications of high social standing; suffect consulships, or
failure to reach the office altogether, and membership of
priesthoods recently devised, like the Sodales Augustales, or
resuscitated, like the Fetiales, go to newcomers. The gradations
and innovations show the Senate defending itself against the
cheapening of privilege and the Princeps satisfying the thirst for
honours amongst new families.

Even without the intervention of the Princeps, the Senate
would have held many more men who had no senatorial antecedents
than it had under the Republic; but fewer of them would have risen
as high as they did. In bringing on these men the Princeps was
acting no differently from the grandees of the Republic who had
their protégés and expected loyal support in return. How he helped
individuals will be discussed in the following three sections.

3.   Elections and appointments

It was a significant part of Augustus' claim to have
returned politics to normality that he 'revived the ancient
privileges of electoral assemblies' ('comitiorum quoque pristinum

ius reduxit'). To back up the original gesture he tried to put a stop to bribery, and so make the game fair for all, by imposing a multiple fine and (rather more questionably) by distributing to the two tribes to which he belonged a thousand sesterces a man on the day of the elections. Whenever he took part in the election of magistrates, he went the round of the tribes with his candidates and appealed for them in the traditional manner, and cast his vote in his tribe, as one of the ordinary electorate. (16)

This evidence alone makes clear that Augustus supported some candidates as an open canvasser. Other men, it is equally clear from the sources, were discouraged from standing. How was it done? The view that Augustus and his successors had some legally confirmed power which guaranteed success to men he supported ('commendatio' used to be interpreted in that sense) has had to be abandoned. Nor did the Princeps exercise influence in virtue of his consular powers, as if he were some kind of third consul responsible for holding the elections and so able to control them. (The consul himself could exercise only limited control: when he presided over an election that was likely to be won by a man he opposed, it seems to have turned into a battle of wills, or of opposing gangs, and the tougher man won.) Rather the Princeps used his influence and his money like any republican politician. But the Princeps' threats, bribes, and promises would loom larger than those of any other politician in the eyes of candidates and electorate. (17)

Even so, Augustus found these methods inadequate to guarantee order in years of crisis or fierce competition. The legislation against bribery of 18 B.C., stories of his occasionally declaring elections invalid and appointing magistrates himself, betray that fact. In A.D.5, perhaps with a view to the peace of mind of his successor, he took a tentative step towards restricting the freedom of the assembly that elected praetors and consuls. There was nothing disreputable about it. The Lex Valeria Cornelia simply created ten new centuries of senators and leading knights which were to act as centuriae praerogativae, giving a strong lead to the remaining centuries of lower social rank. (18)

The new measure did not end electoral disturbances, and in his influential political testament Augustus suggested that the Senate itself should preselect the successful candidates in all the regular electoral contests, leaving the assembly merely to ratify their choice. The senators were pleased: they were to be exempted from courting the people and offering bribes; it was easier and more dignified to make arrangements with the men who were really closely concerned with the outcome of the elections, the candidates' fellow-senators. The new arrangement was put into effect at once, with the praetorian elections of A.D.14. (19) Once again, the dignity of the Senate had been enhanced at the expense of the people's power, but what was done had consequences that neither senators nor perhaps Augustus and Tiberius had expected. Certainly, it became easier for the Princeps to exert pressure on a candidate and his supporters, who were much fewer in numbers than before; moreover it gave the Princeps an active and official role in the elections for the first time, for he seems to have acted as a clearing house for candidacies and presided over the election in the Senate if he were present. On the other hand, the relatively small numbers of men involved in the elections made it possible for candidates themselves and their supporters to strike bargains and make alliances that would guarantee one man office for a given year, his ally for the next. Tiberius frequently had to declare no contest for the consulship; the election had been fixed beforehand, avoiding the humiliation of open failure for those who guessed that their chances of election were not high. (20)

Tacitus passes a savage judgement on Tiberius for these uncontested elections and his invitation to further candidates to present themselves. He is unfair, but it may be that the views of the Princeps, whether known from what he said in the House during or even before the elections or from what could be remembered from past occasions, had more effect than he would have wished. Senators were constantly on the watch for objections to bring against their rivals for posts that were hotly contested, like the praetorship and consulship. Some men might be so intimidated as to give up their ambitions temporarily or permanently: L. Funisulanus Vettonianus was a novus homo of Italian origin who was doing well in the cursus until he commanded the Fourth Legion in Armenia under L. Caesennius Paetus in A.D.62. Caesennius met a humiliating reverse, and Funisulanus, though not in any sense to blame for it as far as we know, did not reach the consulship until some seventeen years after his praetorship. It is not hard to imagine well-wishers reminding him of his misfortune and Nero's conjectured feeling about it. When the time came he may well have enjoyed special encouragement from Vespasian. (21)

Gaius began in 37 with expressions of goodwill and high intent, but he was not long in losing patience with his peers. In 39 he returned elections to the people; that is to say, brought the formal electoral proceedings in the Senate to an end. But he could not unteach the senators how to negotiate with each other. They settled matters between themselves on an informal basis. Soon Gaius had to allow reinstatement of the procedure in the Senate, and that was how things remained. (22)

During the whole Julio-Claudian period, then, the Princeps had to rely on political influence and money to sway the outcome of elections. Nor could he deprive men of rank, nobiles and patricians, of their hereditary prerogatives. Rather he needed to ensure that useful men of lower birth were also qualified by holding the post for the military commands that could follow.

When the Julio-Claudian dynasty ended and the Sabine novus
homo Vespasian came to power at the end of 69 it was no longer
enough for the Princeps to rely on his auctoritas, which was
precisely what Vespasian lacked. Accordingly provision was made in
the 'Lex de Imperio Vespasiani' for his chosen candidates to be
voted on first, so that there could not fail to be room for them
and the Senate would have to vote them down in a yes-no vote if it
did not want them elected: they could not fail of election simply
by getting fewer votes than the other candidates. Even so, the
Emperor could not merely command their success. (23)

Senate and Princeps worked together also for the
appointment of men to posts outside the regular cursus honorum.
For priesthoods, there was a regular procedure by which existing
members nominated candidates; the role of the people in voting for
the candidates was taken over by the Senate. As to com-
missionerships of roads and the like, a man would be proposed in
the Senate, perhaps by the Princeps himself. Inscriptions record
men who are appointed on the suggestion of the Emperor and by
decree of the Senate. Sometimes this was done for appointments to
senatorial provinces too, and the normal method (of drawing lots
between the most senior men qualified) was suspended. P. Paquius
Scaeva, a new man from Histonium on the east coast of Italy, having
once governed Cyprus, was sent back there in the middle years of
Augustus' principate, presumably because the island was in a
disturbed state and needed a man who knew the ground to control it.
But it was a way of putting a country cousin out of competition for
higher office; and when Scaeva returned he found himself put in
charge of suburban roads for a five year period. (24)

The very suspension of the lot might be proposed by the
Princeps. In A.D.21, when Africa had been troubled for several
years by the rebel Tacfarinas, Tiberius wrote to the Senate warning
it that Africa needed a sound military man (a serious snub to the
ex-consuls who were due to draw lots for it). The Princeps left
the choice of the individual to the Senate, but it was remitted to
him once more. Tiberius compromised by offering the House a choice
of two men, one of whom declined to stand. (25)

Even when the lot was operating, the Princeps was not
without influence. Tiberius declined a proposal, made after a
vicious case of extortion had been tried in the Senate, that he
should vet candidates for the proconsulships, but in A.D.35 he
suggested to C. Galba that he should not put himself forward,
probably because he thought he would use the year in wealthy Asia
to recoup his fortunes. Galba killed himself. Much later Domitian
sent emissaries to Cn. Iulius Agricola to intimate that he should
not stand for Asia; there was nothing for it but to take the hint.
(26)

Many posts of real power and high prestige were in the Princeps' direct gift, requiring only formal senatorial sanction for their conferment. Most important, the governorships of provinces entrusted to Augustus in 27 B.C. and when exchanges were made or new provinces acquired. The new province of Egypt always went to an eques, but Syria was governed by an imperial legate who had held the consulship, selected by the Princeps (the appointment was ratified by the Senate) and enjoying imperium delegated to him. The same applied to the greater part of Spain and eventually to commands on the Rhine and in the Balkans. Lesser governorships, open to legates of praetorian standing, were in the Princeps' gift in the same way: so Agricola was sent to Aquitania by Vespasian between praetorship and consulship. The consular legates controlled armies, or at least legions; the subordinate officers, legionary legates and tribunes (except for 24 tribunes still elected by the people under Augustus) and the officers of the two legions controlled by the proconsuls of Africa and Macedonia (until the Macedonian legion was handed over to the imperial legate of Moesia and the African legion put under separate imperial command) were likewise the appointees of the Princeps. (27)

Military distinction, under the Principate as in the Republic, was one of the sure ways to a successful career. But now, with virtually all 'military' posts at the disposal of the Princeps, a man must be known to be loyal as well as distinguished. The first decades of Augustus' principate exhibit few men of consular family in charge of legions: they appear only after his regime was deeply entrenched, in the last fifteen years before Christ. Even so, there was still room for new men of the type of P. Sulpicius Quirinius of Lanuvium, cos. 12 B.C., the 'Cyrenius' who is governor of Syria in St. Luke's Gospel and who may be taken as a paradigm of the most successful novus homo. Describing his brilliant career, Tacitus attributes his advance to a combination of energetic soldiering with eager service. (28)

The imperial monopoly of military posts (as it became by the end of Gaius' reign) has led modern scholars to draw a distinction not noticed by the ancients; but their conception of the 'career in the Emperor's service' has not been helpful. The real distinction is the old republican one: some men's interests and ambitions led them to seek advancement through military service (men like Cn. Iulius Agricola), and others, although they did their due turn as military tribune at the beginning of their careers, were most at home in the Senate or the courts (men like Pliny the Younger, a loyal servant of the Princeps if ever there was one). Professor E.Birley argued that men were selected for 'careers in the Emperor's service' very early in life, when they were holding their first military or civilian posts at the age of about eighteen. He noticed a correlation between the kind of civilian post held at that age and the later career. But what made that distinction was not military talent discerned by the Princeps at an extraordinarily early age, but social distinction. The minor magistracy often held by youths apparently singled out by the Emperor for his service (membership of a four-man commission charged with care of the streets) was in fact obtained by young men of equestrian stock, who had to make their way by merit, since they could not count on the privileges of birth; and merit at Rome, they knew, had always meant military merit above all. (29)

Another reason for rejecting the conception of a special 'career in the Emperor's service' is that it obscures the fact that Emperors had a considerable part to play in bringing men to 'domestic' magistracies, to the governorships of unarmed provinces, and to the new posts devised to deal with administrative problems that under the Republic had been neglected or left to private enterprise: commissions for roads, the Tiber, corn distribution, the water supply, and so on, most of which went to senators of praetorian standing.

Acknowledging the excellence of Tiberius' regime during his early years, Tacitus remarks that his choice of men for office took into account high birth, military distinction, and brilliance in the arts of civil life. (30) Men of military distinction we have already considered; orators and jurisconsults had always held a high place (though second to that of the soldiers) in Roman esteem, and they often put their talents at the disposal of their political allies. Even the Princeps would need advice in drafting legislation and eloquence to support it through the House. Those who collaborated could expect high honours.

Oratory forensic and political had been a prime means of advancement under the Republic: it brought men immediately into the public eye. Under the Empire young men continued to make their forensic début in the centumviral court, as did Pliny the Younger; later they performed before the Senate, and so very often before the Emperor. The change that overtook oratory under the Principate is the subject of Tacitus' Dialogus, and the conclusion drawn was that political tranquillity had deadened the art. From the Princeps' point of view, the choice of brief and the purport of a speech were as important as learning and eloquence.

4.   Prosecutions and enrichment

Cicero had won friends and influence by defending accused men. Even when he sought to accuse Verres he insisted that the action was a defence - of Verres' victims. It had always been acceptable for a young man just embarking on his career to attack a well-known figure, not only for the fame that success brought and the gratia to be had from the man's political enemies, but for the political spoils he would win, sometimes also the financial rewards. But for one established senator to prosecute another, unless he had a known and substantial grievance or acted in self-defence, was not well thought of. That was a feeling that persisted into the Empire. (31)

During the late Republic and early Empire men from a wider circle than ever before could think of entering political life. Unless these <u>domi nobiles</u> from Italy and the provinces enjoyed powerful patronage, they had little to commend them. A successful prosecution was an obvious way of attracting imperial and senatorial attention. Nor would aspirants necessarily be well off; there were young men, some of high rank, others of equestrian stock, whose families had lost their property in civil wars or proscriptions. With fortunes to be won back, perhaps old scores to settle, one might expect an increase in the number of prosecutions; and feuds might perpetuate themselves. The notorious career of M. Aquilius Regulus, Pliny the Younger's enemy, seems to have begun as an attempt to avenge the ruin of Regulus' exiled father and to repair the family fortunes. Before he was old enough to hold the quaestorship, in the last years of Nero, Regulus prosecuted three consulars, winning cash rewards and a priesthood; two of his victims had contributed to his father's downfall. (32)

Another fact that made it more attractive to undertake prosecutions was that success had become more likely under the Principate. Already in the reign of Augustus the most serious cases were beginning to be heard in the Senate itself (see above, p.48). There would be no split between senatorial and equestrian jurymen as sometimes happened in the established jury courts. Moreover, most senators would unite to protect the position of the Princeps, or the legislation he had backed; they could not afford to do anything else. Most important of all was <u>maiestas</u>, the majesty of the Roman state, a concept as elastic as the idea of what might damage it. Under the Principate it covered the Princeps in virtue of his magisterial powers and came to include his kin; the Senate also developed <u>maiestas</u> which had to be protected. By the end of Augustus' principate the 'diminution of majesty' included libels on leading men and women. When he was deified in September A.D.14 it was the signal for further attempts to create new offences by interpretation: in A.D. 15 the former governor of Bithynia, Granius Marcellus, was charged because he was said to have placed his own effigy above those of the Caesars and replaced the head of Augustus' statue with that of Tiberius. The prosecution failed, but ingenuity did not stop there. (33)

Pecuniary penalties made the prosecutions more attractive to the Princeps and more likely to result in conviction. The State Treasury had long been inadequate to Rome's needs; but now the Princeps, not only the Senate and its officials, would bear the opprobrium for its failings. Augustus suffered from these problems, and Tiberius reacted by being notoriously careful of money. Eventually he began to be known as a confiscator, of mines in Spain for example. Under Gaius, Claudius, and Nero wealthy men were never entirely safe from a speculative accuser who would get his reward and provide a lump sum to the state. One success could tempt a man to go on to try his luck again. L. Fulcinius Trio, cos. suff. 31, is a case in point. He joined in the attack on Libo Drusus in 16, and was rewarded by the Senate with a share of Libo's property and a praetorship extra ordinem. Four years later he saw another golden opportunity: the impending trial of Cn. Piso for extortion in Spain, the murder of Germanicus Caesar, and a treasonable attempt to re-enter his province of Syria by violence. On this occasion his reward was Tiberius' promise of support when he stood for further office - coupled with a warning against excessive vehemence in his oratory. (34)

Scholarly attention has focused on maiestas and its abuse, especially under Tiberius and his successors. But the state of affairs in the Forum near the beginning of Tiberius' reign was already being loudly deplored in the Senate by L. Piso, and he was not thinking of maiestas but rather of malicious prosecution under the Lex Papia Poppaea of A.D.9 which regulated the right of the unmarried and childless to succeed to property, and perhaps of the abuse of other statutes as well. (35) For an attack in the Senate, no statute at all was required: the Senate could take cognizance of what it chose. In A.D.21 Clutorius Priscus was brought before it for reciting his poem on the death of Drusus Caesar, he being still alive. The charge has caused difficulty; probably there was none, beyond the recitation of the poem. M. Lepidus drew attention to that when he proposed that Priscus should suffer banishment, the penalty that Lepidus said he would have proposed if the charge had been maiestas. The Senate did not take the point, and voted for execution. (36)

Attempts were made to remedy abuses, usually at the beginning of a principate. The Emperor might be induced to renounce maiestas, for example; so with Gaius, Claudius, and (tacitly) Nero. (37) What that meant is not clear. Not the repeal of the Lex, which was never re-enacted; nor did the Senate suspend the statute; the state could not do without it. Rather perhaps (as Professor Brunt has suggested to me) the Princeps undertook not to entertain charges of slander or libel under that statute. Even in the middle of Tiberius' principate, after one inept prosecution, the Senate debated how to prevent another such being brought. The solution that appealed to them (it shows the way their minds were working) was to withhold the rewards offered to prosecutors, if the accused man killed himself before conviction. Tiberius would not allow it. His refusal did his reputation no good, but it was not necessarily motivated by malice or fear. The method of private prosecution was long established, the rewards guaranteed by law. As to the Lex Papia Poppaea, all that Tiberius did about the abuse of that statute was to set up a senatorial commission to clarify its provisions (A.D. 20). In Nero's reign, however, there was an effort to lessen the inducement to prosecute under it: the reward was limited to one quarter the sum involved. (38)

In the main it is reasonable to hold the Princeps of the day responsible for these abuses, though the issues in each prosecution might be very marginal to his interests, or not concern him at all. Gaius Caligula's backer Q. Naevius Sutorius Macro, Prefect of the Guard after the fall of Sejanus in 31, launched attacks on Gaius' potential rivals towards the end of Tiberius' reign. In one of the last, that on L. Arruntius (another man judged to be capax imperii, and an influential friend of the Princeps), Tiberius is said not even to have known what was going on. But it was the duty of the Princeps to know, and a mockery of senatorial freedom to allow abusive prosecutions to continue. And there were a number of cases throughout the Julio-Claudian period either instigated by the Princeps himself or involving his participation. (39)

Riches were a real if unacknowledged aim of Roman politicians, and historians deplored avaritia as one of the prevailing vices leading to the fall of the Republic. It is true that provincial governors, especially those in provinces that were economically advanced or those who had the chance of easy victories and plunder, could see how life might be lived and found the means of achieving luxury and wealth temptingly close at hand. But the cost of rising in the cursus was great, and remained so even when popular election was abolished in A.D. 14. Senators were still under continuous pressure to keep up with their peers. Old families were in competition with nouveaux riches from Italy and provinces, and their wealth was largely tied up in land. From the reign of Augustus we hear of the poverty of individual (long established) senatorial families, and in the reign of Claudius a complaint of the poverty of Italian senators in general or, more especially, of senators from Latium. Libo Drusus, who allegedly conspired against Tiberius and his sons in A.D. 16, was a man of much less ability and vigour than Catiline; but both were aiming at the highest position in the state without having the means to support their claims. (40)

The poverty of senators gave additional power to the Princeps: he could relieve it or force them to give up their seats. They sometimes let their resentment be seen. Augustus paid a man's debts and received a brief letter of thanks: 'Nothing for me'. Then there was M. Hortalus, grandson of the great orator Hortensius, who brought his children to the door of the Senate-house in A.D. 16 and pointed out that it was Augustus who had encouraged him to produce them. Finally a praetor under Nero, A. Fabricius Veiento, who found himself unable to pay the exorbitant prizes demanded by charioteers and began to train dogs instead. But Veiento's impudence towards his peers, which was to get him exiled from Italy and his books burnt, suggests that he was more concerned to show up the extortion than to save his purse. At any rate he was successful: Nero himself paid the difference. (41)

Poverty also embittered competition for remunerative posts. The proconsulship of Asia was sought not only for its prestige but for profit as well, as the number of prosecutions brought by its inhabitants shows. Tacitus' account of senatorial politics during the early twenties reveals senior consulars playing some ingenious and dirty tricks in their efforts to bring forward their own turn for Asia. (42)

There were other ways of making money. Legacy hunting was a sport open to all Romans, requiring only social skill; but the successful bringing of charges under the Lex Papia Poppaea and other statutes required oratorical talent. Not only criminal charges were a source of profit. A practice at the civil bar could be lucrative. In 17 B.C. Augustus had revived the Lex Cincia against taking fees for advocacy, but it was easy to evade, and advocates would receive handsome gifts and bequests. (43)

The overt role of money in political life under the Julio-Claudians is well illustrated by the case of Aemilia Lepida, charged in A.D. 20 with falsely claiming to have had a child by P. Sulpicius Quirinius, cos. 12 B.C. Their marriage had long since ended, and Quirinius was now an old man near death. The name of Lepida's prosecutor is not given by Tacitus, so he was probably an obscure person. But he must have been either a beneficiary under Quirinius' will or put up by him to prevent it being overturned in favour of the child; Tiberius had done something similar for the benefit of two members of the aristocracy, one of them perhaps the brother of Lepida, who was her counsel in 20. (44)

The trial of Lepida is interesting for another reason: the favour shown her by the people, when she appeared in the theatre. Their formal role in political life was now minimal and their unwelcome intervention usually took the form of demonstrations when the grain supply failed and riots between the partisans of various theatrical performers. But they showed consistent loyalty and affection towards certain members of the imperial family, and their sympathy with a member of the Republican aristocracy dealing with a well-heeled parvenu may have given Lepida and her friends some comfort.

Fear of poverty probably lies behind two debates on senatorial extravagance reported by Tacitus. One came in 16, immediately after the condemnation of Libo Drusus. Money had been one of his preoccupations, and it was a good moment to lighten the burden of competition by tightening up the rules against the use of gold plate at dinner parties. Some senators tried unsuccessfully to make the House go further and forbid silver vessels and silk garments for men. There was another debate in 22, initiated by the aediles, who would not have acted without having strong support. It is quite clear that social and political competition was leading senators into expenditure many of them could not afford and which they feared would attract the attention of an austere and parsimonious Princeps. They no longer had to win the vote of the people, but their fellow senators had to be impressed, treated, and perhaps paid off. On top of that, magistrates still had to provide games for the people; if they were deficient, peers as well as people would take note. In 22, Tiberius told the Senate that there were already statutes on the subject of extravagance which were being ignored; he would not add to them. The remedy was in the senators' own hands: their self-respect. (45)

Eleven years later the Princeps was forced to act, not against extravagance, but to relieve an acute shortage of cash: senators could not meet their debts. Only a substantial injection of capital from the imperial purse brought the crisis to an end. It did nothing to solve the long-term problem: want of ready money and realisable assets must have kept many men out of active politics, or forced them to leave it, quite apart from those whose capital fell below the requisite value. (46)

5.   Senatorial indifference

In spite of the swollen size of the Senate at the beginning of the Principate, Augustus and some of his successors had difficulty in filling certain posts. First, the minor magistracies held before entry to the Senate with the quaestorship. During the last decade but one of the first century B.C. Augustus had to reduce the number of posts available at this level from 26 to 20, the same number as quaestorships. Even that was not enough, and we find men holding these posts as part of an equestrian set, so little competition was there from would-be senators. The Principes did not care for these signs of apathy: Claudius' prospective sons-in-law had to hold the minor magistracies. (47)

There was also a shortage of candidates for tribuneship and aedileship in the early Principate. Already in 33 B.C. we hear of an aedileship being filled by M. Agrippa, who was an ex-consul. His aedilician games helped to win Octavian popularity before the struggle with Antony, but there may already have been a shortage of candidates for the post. In 13 B.C. it was the tribunate that failed to attract enough candidates, so that Augustus forced ex-quaestors of less than forty years of age to draw lots for the posts; when the same problem arose again the following year knights were encouraged to stand without committing themselves to membership of the Senate. Claudius found himself in similar difficulties, and solved them in the same way as Augustus had in 12 B.C. (48)

During the principate of Augustus there was still a high proportion of patricians in the Senate, 29% according to de Laet. They were debarred from holding plebeian offices, so that the only posts open to them at the stage of tribunate and aedileship would have been the curule aedileships, two posts out of the sixteen available. To make them queue up for those would have created an intolerable bottleneck for the socially most distinguished group of men in the Senate; instead, patricians were exempted altogether from holding the posts and could pass straight from quaestorship to praetorship, giving them an advantage that none at Rome would begrudge their rank.

But these posts had in truth lost their intrinsic attract- iveness. The career of Julius Caesar illustrates the value of aedileship under the Republic as a means of winning support for further office by giving games for the people – an expensive business. Under the Principate, in particular after the abolition of popular elections, the support of the Emperor was more important. The tribunate also declined in the face of Augustus' tribunicia potestas; when in 66 a tribune offered to veto the proceedings in the Senate that were to lead to the death of Thrasea Paetus, the victim rejected the offer as dangerous and futile. It was only in the Flavio-Trajanic age, when the cursus was pursued by eager new men brought in from an ever-widening circle of provinces, that the tribunate became a post to be canvassed for. (49)

Even for the highest positions the Emperor Tiberius complained of a dearth of applicants. He was writing of the governorships of provinces, more precisely in connexion with the legateship of Syria, in A.D. 32. It may be that Tiberius' standards were too high and so his choice of candidates limited, but he may well have had the experience of approaching a qualified candidate and being refused. (50) Already in the late Republic Cicero had been reluctant to proceed to Cilicia. For him, political success and emoluments were to be had at Rome; many senators may have felt the same under the Principate.

At Rome there was slackness in attending senatorial meetings. Augustus dealt with it by establishing fixed days for meetings and setting the quorum at a realistic figure which might make the conscientious bring pressure to bear on their less eager peers. (51)

All this indicates indifference to the senatorial career on the part of some politicians, either at the initial stages, so that they declined to embark on the cursus at all, or at certain later stages; all those ex-quaestors under forty (they could have been sitting in the House for fifteen years) must have been content to be passive back-benchers (pedarii); others, who had attained the highest domestic posts, were unwilling to give up the metropolis for a spell (under Tiberius perhaps a long spell) in the provinces.

For individual instances of failure to play a full part in
political life a different range of factors may be in question:
poverty, incapacity, laziness, caution, quietism, indifference,
cynicism - and high indignation with the new scheme of things.
This last, however, would take the form of unmistakable political
action, not half-hearted participation. Cn. Piso and L. Sestius,
coss. suff. in 23 B.C., had pointedly abstained from standing for
the consulship; when they reversed their policy it was not to do
the Princeps a favour or because he invited them; rather it was to
lead a movement for greater independence and initiative on the part
of the Senate. That had come to be out of the question by A.D. 59:
all Thrasea Paetus could do when Agrippina the Younger was murdered
by her son Nero was to walk out of the House. In the end, one of
the charges against him was that the whole empire was agog to read
the usually dreary official accounts of public events to see which
ones he had boycotted. (52) Every polity offers its members a
range of action within which they are expected to keep; that
available under the Principate to the senatorial class was
relatively narrow.

The only effective way for a politician to challenge the
basis of the new regime was by force. But no military revolt
against the Julio-Claudians proved effective until Nero lost
control of the Praetorian Guard; very few were even attempted.
Augustus, Tiberius, and Germanicus had been too successful in
yoking the loyalty of the soldiers to their dynasty. The only
practical remedy was assassination. Yet in the first two hundred
years of the Principate, only Gaius, Domitian and Commodus died
that way, and only in the first murder did senators play an active
part.

Senators had a further and particular reason for dis-
illusionment and resentment under the Principate. If politics was
the pursuit of fame, power and wealth, it could be practised
elsewhere than in the House, and the objects obtained directly from
the Princeps. This was observed by those who abstained from
seeking senatorial honours and who instead accepted offices open to
equites. The most distinguished or most favoured could become
Prefects of Egypt or of the Praetorian Guard like Sejanus, Macro,
and Afranius Burrus. Tacitus claimed that it was Sejanus who gave
access to the consulship in the twenties; but even the lesser
equestrian posts could be almost as prestigious and much more
remunerative than what an ordinary senator might hope for. So
thought Seneca's brother Annaeus Mela when he decided on
procuratorships against the cursus honorum. (53) The prefectures,
as official military posts, enjoyed a standing of their own, while
the procuratorships were domestic posts of the Princeps. That did
not matter for long, because by the reign of Claudius the Princeps
was no longer a private individual who held this power and that
(privatus cum imperio), but an Emperor, whose powers were conferred
en bloc and used without enquiry as to which exactly was being

deployed on each occasion. If the Emperor was no longer a private person, his servants were now officials, and the title of procurator became acceptable for governors of provinces. (54)

Further, the imperial power was virtually hereditary, and conferred official standing on other members of the imperial family, notably the wives and mothers of Emperors. Their servants and friends became courtiers and politicians. By the same token, freedmen of the Emperor and his immediate family could wield immense power, not only because a few positions within the imperial household enabled them to control machinery of state (the man who was in charge of the Emperor's purses, the a rationibus, is the prime example: he was able to exercise effective control over the finances of the whole empire), but much more because of the influence that their closeness to the Emperor gave them: from them he sought disinterested advice, precisely because they were not politicians in the conventional sense; and their patronage earned them vast wealth as well as power. (55)

All this was bitterly resented by members of the Senate. As a body they had to acknowledge it by conferring the insignia of high senatorial rank on the most successful of the upstarts: ornamenta consularia on Prefects of the Guard from Sejanus onwards; later even procurators might be granted them; and the insignia of praetor and quaestor were conferred respectively on Pallas and Narcissus, the most powerful of the freedmen in their heyday, the reigns of Claudius and Nero. (56) Later Emperors were more cautious in acknowledging their debt to freedmen, but the Principate did not become less autocratic as time went on, and the Emperor's household and equestrian 'friends' could not but exercise more power than senatorial politicians wished. The only solace was that anyone who entered the politics of the court had to reckon on its dangers, as Sejanus, Mela, Burrus, Narcissus, and Pallas all found: loss of post, disgrace, even death.

6. Conclusion

The resilience and conservatism of senatorial politics were tempered by powerful forces for change. Not the least important factor was the rapid turnover in personnel. It is hard to find families established in the House when Caesar crossed the Rubicon who are still secure during the reign of Vespasian. This has often been noticed; the core of it is 'the doom of the nobiles', in Sir Ronald Syme's striking phrase. The Principate was destructive, both in the way it became established and in the way it maintained itself. Its victims were not all executed or exiled. Some withdrew (see above, pp.61-2). There were those families too which found that they could not afford to send even one representative to the senate in each generation, or which, by miscalculating, failed to reproduce themselves in sufficient numbers to keep going at all. Impoverishment was often a consequence of the Roman revolution, direct or indirect (see above, pp.58-60).

But there is a danger of painting too lurid a picture. Much of our evidence comes from the writings of Tacitus, Suetonius, and Cassius Dio, who are concerned with what was striking or historically significant, with men in the forefront of political life. Behind these champions may lie a mass of men whose families sustained the shocks of Dictatorship, Civil War, Triumvirate, and evolving Principate. They kept quiet, but they may have helped to carry on a tradition.

The great issue of the late Republic, that of political supremacy in the state, had been fought and lost by the generation of Cicero and Cato. What remained to decide was how to stand in face of the new power: whether to defy, accept, or exploit it. Major decisions were out of the Senate's hands, not even all the positions of power were open to senators. That gave greater prominence to the contest for place and dignity that had always been important in Roman politics. The focus of major struggles was the favour of the Princeps and his favourites; for the foresighted, the favour of his presumptive heirs. They were fought with familiar weapons: electoral pacts, marriage alliances, denigration, and the political trial, which now had a deadlier edge. The balance of power between Princeps and Senate changed continuously but irregularly, for his position as a whole was neither enshrined in the constitution nor much restricted by it. Until a point of rest was reached – perhaps by the end of Domitian's reign – senators had a duty not to waste their political time by attending too much to their own interest as individuals, by opportunism or quietism. On the whole they did not fulfil it. When equilibrium was reached, the days of the Senate as a corporate political force were over.

Notes

1.   Dio LIII 30 - LIV 12;   Vell. Pat. II 91.2ff; see B.Levick, Greece and Rome 22 (1975) 156ff, with bibliography, n.1.

2.   Corvinus: Suet. Div. Aug. 58; see R.Syme, History in Ovid (Oxford 1978), index. M. Lepidus: R.Syme, JRS 45 (1955) 22ff, repr. in Ten Studies in Tacitus (Oxford 1970).

3.   Afer: Tac. Ann. IV 52; 66.1; Paetus: XIV 12.2, cf. XVI 24.1f; Priscus: Hist. IV 6ff; 43; Suet. Div. Vesp. 15; Dio LXVI 12B. Change: Tac. Ann. III 55.4.

4. B.Levick, _Tiberius the Politician_ (London 1976) 92ff
    (Tiberius); 148ff (twenties); 201ff (Gaius); D.Timpe,
    Untersuchungen zur Kontinuität des frühen Prinzipats,
    Hist.Einzelschr. 5 (Wiesbaden 1962) 94ff.

5. The 700: _Res Gestae Divi Aug._ 25.3; _lectio_ of 29: Suet. _Div._
    Aug. 35; Dio LII 42.1ff; 18 B.C.: Suet. _loc.cit._ and 54; Dio
    LIV 13.1ff; A.D.4: LV 13.3f. See A.H.M.Jones, 'The Censorial
    Powers of Augustus,', _Studies_ 21ff. For the lower age limit
    see G.V.Sumner, _Latomus_ 26 (1967) 413ff. Note that Keith
    Hopkins, _Death and Renewal_ 146f, uses the 600-man Senate as
    one co-ordinate in an enquiry into senators' expectation of
    life. On the difficulties that a Senate as small as 300 would
    have caused, see R.J.A.Talbert, _Greece and Rome_ 31 (1984) 55f.

6. Suet. _Div. Aug._ 41.1; Dio LIV 17,3, cf.30.2; see C.Nicolet,
    JRS 66 (1976) 20ff. For the dress assumed by prospective
    senators, see Talbert, _op.cit._ 56.

7. Vell. Pat. II 89.3. F.Millar, _JRS_ 63 (1973) 50ff, fails to
    give due weight to the change that took place in 27 B.C.

8. Legislation: see G.Rotondi, _Leges Publicae Populi Romani_
    (Milan 1922) 441ff. _Senatus Consulta_: W.Kunkel, _An_
    Introduction to Roman Legal and Constitutional History (ed.2,
    tr. J.Kelly, Oxford 1973) 125ff.

9. See J.Bleicken, _Senatsgericht und Kaisergericht_ (Göttingen,
    1962); A.H.M.Jones, 'Imperial and Senatorial Jurisdiction in
    the Early Principate', _Studies_ 69ff; _Criminal Courts of the_
    Roman Republic and Principate (Oxford 1972) 90ff. (to be used
    with caution). Claudius: Tac. _Ann._ XIII 4.2.

10. Princeps as source of law: Kunkel, _op.cit._ 127ff. The
    Committee: Dio LIII 21.4; Suet. _Div. Aug._ 35.3; see J.Crook,
    Consilium Principis (Cambridge 1955) 8ff. Change of A.D. 13:
    Dio LVI 28.2f. Nero: Tac. _Ann._ XIII 26.2; XIV 49.2.

11. Dio LV 24.9ff. It was Mr. R.Nowell-Smith who drew my atten-
    tion to the significance of this reference to Caesar.

12. Tiberius: Tac. _Ann._ III 65.3; Claudius: BGU 611 = Smallwood,
    Docs. 367, _fin._; Nero: Tac. _Ann._ XIII 49; Gauls: XI 23.

13. Tac. _Ann._ III 53f.

14. New men: see T.P.Wisemen, _New Men in the Roman Senate 139 B.C._
    _- A.D. 14_ (Oxford 1971) 184ff. Paelignian: _ILS_ 932 = Ehrenberg
    and Jones, _Docs._ 205. For the 'highly permeable' Senate, see
    K.Hopkins, _Death and Renewal_ 31ff. Praetorships: Vell. Pat.

II 89.3, and Dio LIII 32.2 (10, 23 B.C.); LVI 25.4 (16, A.D. 11, cf. Tac. Ann. I 14.6, A.D. 14); Dio LVIII 20.5 (15-16, A.D. 33 onwards); LIX 20.5 (the same, A.D. 39 onwards); Pomponius in Dig. I 2. 2. 32 (two added by Claudius). Quarrelling: Tac. Ann. XIV 28.1.

15. M.Gelzer, The Roman Nobility (trans. R.Seager, Oxford 1975) 141ff; P.A.Brunt, JRS 51 (1961) 74ff, and 72 (1982) 1ff.

16. Lex de ambitu: Dio LIV 16.1, and other texts cited by Rotondi, op.cit. 443, including Suet. Div. Aug. 40.2 (distributions); for canvassing, 56.2.

17. Deterrence: Dio LV 22.1 (Cinna); commendatio: B.Levick, Historia 16 (1967) 207ff; A.L.Astin, Latomus 28 (1969) 863ff. Power of consul: B.Levick, Athenaeum 59 (1981) 378ff.

18. Appointment: Dio LIV 10.2 (19 B.C.); LV 34.1 (A.D. 7); cf. Suet. Nero 43. Measure of A.D.5: Ehrenberg and Jones, Docs. 94a and b; P.A.Brunt, JRS 51 (1961) 71ff.

19. Vell. Pat. II 124.3f, with A.J.Woodman ad loc.; Tac. Ann. I 15.1f.

20. Tac. Ann. I 81.

21. Tac. Ann. XV 7.2; ILS 1005.

22. Dio LIX 20.3ff.

23. For the 'Lex de Imperio Vespasiani', see Ehrenberg and Jones, Docs. 364, with P.A.Brunt, JRS 67 (1977) 95ff, and, on the fourth clause, B.Levick, Historia 16 (1967) 210f.

24. Ehrenberg and Jones, Docs. 197.

25. Tac. Ann. III 32.1; 35.

26. Tac. Agr. 42.1ff.

27. Provinces divided: Strabo III p.839f.; Dio LIII 11ff, with A.H.M.Jones, A History of Rome through the Fifth Century II (London etc. 1970) 25ff. Agricola: Tac. Agr. 9.1. Tribuni militum a populo: Lawrence Keppie, The Making of the Roman Army (London 1984) 178. Africa: J.P.V.D.Balsdon, The Emperor Gaius (Oxford 1937) 154f.; Macedonia: R.Syme, Danubian Papers (Bucharest 1971) 50ff.

28. See P.A.Brunt, JRS 51 (1961) 73, n.13. Quirinius: Tac. Ann. III 48.

29. E.Birley, Brit. Acad. Proc. 39 (1953) 197ff; cf. D.McAlindon, JRS 47 (1957) 191ff.

30. Tac. Ann. IV 6.2.

31. See L.R.Taylor, Party Politics in the Age of Caesar (Berkeley etc. 1961) 98ff; A.N.Sherwin-White on Pliny Ep. I 5.1; R.Syme, Tacitus (Oxford 1958), I 323ff; B.Levick, Tiberius the Politician (London 1976) 189ff.

32. Tac. Hist. IV 42; Pliny Ep. I 5, with Sherwin-White ad loc.

33. See R.Bauman, The Crimen Maiestatis (Johannesburg 1967), and Impietas in Principem (Munich 1974); B.Levick, Tiberius 183ff, with bibliography. Granius: Tac. Ann. I 74.

34. Tac. Ann. III 18.2; cf. IV 20.2; VI 19.1; Suet. Tib. 49 (Tiberius); Cal. 38 (Gaius); Tac. Ann. XI 1, mentioning 'opes principibus infensas', XVI 17.4f (Nero). Trio: Tac. Ann. II 28, 30.1; III 10.1f; 19.1.

35. Tac. Ann. II 34.1f. Lex Papia Poppaea: III 25ff, with Furneaux ad loc.; Dio LVI 10.3.

36. Tac. Ann. III 49ff.

37. Bauman, Impietas 191ff.

38. Tac. Ann. IV 28ff. Lex Papia Poppaea: III 25.6; Suet. Nero 10.

39. Arruntius: Tac. Ann. VI 47f; capax: I 13.2. Macro: Levick, Tiberius 201ff.

40. Avaritia: see, e.g., Sall. Cat. 10. Poverty: Tac. Ann. XI 23.5f. Libo: II 27.2.

41. Imperial subventions: Res Gest. App. 4; Tac. Ann. I 75.5f; II 37; 48.3; XIII 34.2; Sen. De Ben. II 7.2, 27.2; Ep. 122.10; Dio LIV 17.3; LV 13.7; LVII 10.3f. The letter: Macr. Sat. II 23. Hortalus: Tac. Ann. II 37. Veiento: Dio LXI 6.2f; cf. Tac. Ann. XIV 50.

42. Tac. Ann. III 32; 58; 69.1; 71.3f.

43. Dio LIV 18.2; Tac. Ann. XI 5f, with Furneaux ad loc.

44. Tac. Ann. III 22f; Suet. Tib. 49, with G.B.Townend, Latomus 21 (1962) 484ff. The earlier inheritances: Tac. Ann. II 48.1ff.

45. Tac. Ann. II 33f, III 52ff. For gladiatorial games, see K.Hopkins, Death and Renewal 7f.

46. Tac. Ann. VI 16ff., with C.Rodewald, Money in the Age of Tiberius (Manchester 1976) 1ff., and E. Lo Cascio, JRS 68 (1978) 201f.

47. Dio LIV 26.5ff. Equites: see, e.g., Ehrenberg and Jones, Docs. 235; the vigintivirate post is held twice by Paquius Scaeva, ibid. 197; cf. 196 for repeated tenure of the triumvirate capitalis. Claudius: Dio LX 5.8; but cf. Tac. Ann. III 29.1, where Nero Caesar is exempted. For 'withdrawal' see Hopkins, Death and Renewal 166ff.

48. Aedileships: Dio LIII 2.2; LIV 11.2. Agrippa: XLIX 43.1ff. Events of 13-12 B.C: LIV 26.7; 30.2. Claudius: Dio LX 11.8.

49. Patricians: S.J.de Laet, De Samenstelling van den rom. Senaat (Antwerp 1941) 251ff, 323f (French). A.D. 66: Tac. Ann. XVI 26.6. Canvassing: Pliny Ep. II 9.2.

50. Tac. Ann. VI 27.3.

51. Suet. Div. Aug. 35.3; cf. Dio LX 11.8, for compulsory at-tendance under Claudius. Retiring age: D.McAlindon, Class.Rev. 7 (1957) 108; R.J.A.Talbert, Greece and Rome 31 (1984) 58.

52. Reluctance to enter the Senate: Dio LIV 26.4. Sestius and Piso: LIII 32.4; Tac. Ann. II 43.3. Thrasea: XIV 12.2; XVI 21f.

53. Sejanus and the consulship: Tac. Ann. IV 68.2. Mela: XVI 17.3, with his death in 4.

54. See P.A.Brunt, Latomus 25 (1966) 29ff.

55. A rationibus: Tac. Ann. XIII 14.1ff; Statius Silv. III 3.86ff. Nature of freedmen's power: F.Millar, JRS 57 (1967) 14, and Hopkins, Death and Renewal 176ff; for a later parallel, see K.Hopkins, Conquerors and Slaves (Cambridge 1978) 172ff, on eunuchs.

56. Ornamenta: see Taylor, op.cit. 113f. Sejanus: Dio LVII 19.7; Macro: LVIII 12.7; Rufrius Crispinus: Tac. Ann. XI 4.5, cf. XVI 17.2; Burrus: Smallwood, Docs. 259. Procurators: Suet. Div. Claud. 24.1; Dio LX 3; Tac. Ann. XII 21.2. Pallas: 23.2; Narcissus: XI 38.5.

Bibliographical Notes

Introduction

On early Rome, see Tim Cornell in Cornell and Matthews, Atlas of the Roman World (London 1982) 1-38; for Cicero as an 'historian', Elizabeth Rawson, JRS 62 (1970) 33-45; for Livy, P.G.Walsh, Livy: his Historical Aims and Methods (Cambridge 1961) and Livy (Greece and Rome New Surveys, no. 8 1974); for Tacitus, F.R.D.Goodyear, Tacitus (Greece and Rome New Surveys, no. 4 1970), Ronald Martin, Tacitus (London 1981), and above all Ronald Syme, Tacitus (Oxford 1958), especially chapters 21-34 on the Annals.

On political life in the Roman Republic before the Ciceronian age, see Fergus Millar, 'The Political Character of the Classical Roman Republic', JRS 74 (1984) 1 ff.

Competition and Co-operation

The standard work in English on the aristocratic ideology of the Roman Republic is Donald Earl, The Moral and Political Tradition of Rome (London 1967). On monumenta and public display, still as conspicuous as ever in the twenties B.C., see Werner Eck, 'Senatorial Self-representation: Developments in the Augustan Period', in Fergus Millar and Erich Segal (eds.), Caesar Augustus: Seven Aspects (Oxford 1984) 129-167. On the triumph, see A.J.Marshall, 'Symbols and Showmanship in Roman Public Life', Phoenix 38 (1984) 120-41.

For the effects of the ideology, see W.V.Harris, War and Imperialism in Republican Rome (Oxford 1979), especially pp. 17-34 and 117-130; P.A.Brunt, 'Laus imperii', in P.D.A.Garnsey and C.R.Whittaker (eds.), Imperialism in the Ancient World (Cambridge

1978) 159-191, especially pp. 162-4, 168-72; Elizabeth Rawson, 'Caesar's Heritage: Hellenistic Kings and their Roman Equals', JRS 65 (1975) 148-159, especially pp. 152-6. On the late-republican period in particular, the second chapter of Sir Ronald Syme's The Roman Revolution (Oxford 1939) is basic; on the 'military dynasts', see the concluding chapters, respectively, of Ernst Badian, Roman Imperialism in the Late Republic (2nd ed., Oxford 1968), and Michael Crawford, The Roman Republic (Fontana 1978); on the Augustan and early-imperial period, Syme Roman Revolution chapters 26 and 32.

For the question of wealth in the Roman upper-class value system, see W.V.Harris, 'On War and Greed in the Second Century B.C.', American Historical Review 76 (1971) 1371-1385; Israel Shatzman, Senatorial Wealth and Roman Politics (Coll. Latomus 142, Brussels 1975) provides an exhaustive collection of material on how senators got their income and what they spent it on.

On 'parties' and 'factions', see Lily Ross Taylor, Party Politics in the Age of Caesar (California 1949), especially ch.1, and Erich S.Gruen, The Last Generation of the Roman Republic (California 1975), especially ch.2. Both books should be used with caution: on Gruen's overall argument there is an important review by M.H.Crawford in JRS 66 (1976) 214-6. For criticism of particular 'factional' interpretations, see for instance I. Shatzman, 'Scaurus, Marius and the Metelli: a Prosopographical-Factional Case', Ancient Society 5 (1974) 197-222, and T.P.Wiseman, 'Factions and Family Trees', Liverpool Classical Monthly 1 (1976) 1-3. On 'optimates' and 'populares', the best accounts are W.K.Lacey, 'Boni atque improbi', Greece and Rome 17 (1970) 3-16, and Robin Seager, 'Cicero and the Word Popularis', CQ 22 (1972) 328-338; see also G.E.M. de Ste.Croix, The Class Struggle in the Ancient Greek World (London 1981) 352-355.

Matthias Gelzer's The Roman Nobility (Engl. trans. Robin Seager, Oxford 1969) gives a thorough account of political behaviour, packed with detailed examples. Fundamental on particular aspects of co-operation are P.A.Brunt, 'Amicitia in the Late Roman Republic', PCPS n.s. 11 (1965) 1-20 = R.Seager (ed.) The Crisis of the Roman Republic (Cambridge 1969) 199-218, and R.Seager, 'Factio: Some Observations', JRS 62 (1972) 53-58. R.P.Saller, Personal Patronage under the Early Empire (Cambridge 1982) ch.1 is important on the 'reciprocity ethic' and the ideology of patronage. The best short account of Roman senators' attitudes to political issues – concentrating on the late Republic, but applying to other periods too – is P.A.Brunt's review article in JRS 58 (1968) 229-232 (discussing Ch. Meier, Res Publica Amissa).

Politics in the Late Republic

The production of scholarly works on Rome in the Late Republic continues to be enormous. What follows can only represent the tip of the iceberg.

The evidence of the works of Cicero remains crucial. These are widely available in translation in Penguin Classics and Loeb Classical Library. The edition of Cicero's letters by D.R.Shackleton Bailey (Cambridge 1965-78) is outstanding and his Cicero (London 1971) makes extensive use of the sources in translation. The Commentariolum Petitionis (Comm. Pet., 'A Short Guide to Electioneering') is ascribed to Quintus Cicero, the orator's brother. Even if its authorship is in doubt (on which see J.Richardson, Historia 20 (1971) 436ff), it remains invaluable evidence and is available in LACTOR 3 (London Association of Classical Teachers, 1961).

For details of office-holders in Rome see T.R.S. Broughton, The Magistrates of the Roman Republic (New York 1951-60) (MRR). H.H.Scullard, From the Gracchi to Nero (5th ed., London 1982) remains the most useful straightforward account of the period with excellent notes to guide the reader to the relevant specialist literature. More detailed and challenging studies can be found in E.S.Gruen, Roman Politics and the Criminal Courts 149-78 B.C. (Harvard 1968) and his The Last Generation of the Roman Republic (Berkeley 1974). On the structure of Roman society and political life see C.Nicolet, The World of the Citizen in Republican Rome (London 1980).

For the nature of the Roman ruling class, M.Gelzer, The Roman Nobility (Oxford 1969) is fundamental. However there is a danger that modern commentators too readily follow Gelzer and overemphasize the exclusiveness of the inner aristocracy and its hold on the highest offices. For an antidote see now K.Hopkins, Death and Renewal (Cambridge 1983) ch. 2. On 'new men' and how to get on in Roman politics see T.P.Wiseman, New Men in the Roman Senate 139 B.C. - 14 A.D. (Oxford 1971). On the importance of senatorial wealth see I.Shatzman, Senatorial Wealth and Roman Politics (Brussels 1975). For political relationships between members of the ruling class see P.Brunt, 'Amicitia' in the Late Roman Republic', PCPS n.s. 11 (1965) 1ff. (reprinted in R.Seager ed., The Crisis of the Roman Republic (Cambridge 1969).

For the political values and attitudes of the Roman aristocracy, see D.Earl, The Moral and Political Tradition of Rome (London 1967), J.Hellegouarc'h, Le Vocabulaire latin des relations et des parties politiques sous la République (Paris 1963),

G.Achard, Pratique rhétorique et idéologie politique dans les discours 'optimates' de Cicéron (Leiden 1981).

For an understanding of how politics worked in the Republic, L.R.Taylor, Party Politics in the Age of Caesar (Berkeley 1949) still has its uses; but its very title and much of its contents are the antithesis of the arguments presented here. C.Meier, Res republica amissa (Wiesbaden 1966) has much to offer. N.Rouland, Rome, Démocratie Impossible? (Actes Sud 1981) is wild at times, but full of ideas: it is a rather general account of his detailed thesis, Pouvoir politique et dépendance personnelle dans l'Antiquité romaine (Brussels 1979). B.Rawson, The Politics of Friendship (Sydney 1978), while nominally about the relationship between Pompey and Cicero, is one of the clearest and best books about Roman politics in English and makes use of a large quantity of material in translation.

It is inevitable that we know most about the political careers of the leading characters of the Roman Republic. There has been a spate of biographies in recent years which are useful and illuminating provided that it is remembered that Pompey and Caesar and the like are not typical. On Sulla, A.Keaveney, Sulla, The Last Republican (London 1982) provides a sympathetic account; E.Badian, 'Waiting for Sulla' (JRS 52 (1962) 52) is on the other hand fiercely hostile, while still providing a useful, if controversial, analysis of the careers of men in this period. For Pompey's political career in Rome, R.Seager, Pompey, A Political Biography (Oxford 1979) is the clearest and best account. E.Gruen, 'Pompey, the Roman Aristocracy and the conference of Luca', Historia 18 (1969) 71 ff, illuminates the relationship between Pompey and the most influential aristocrats. For M. Crassus, Allen Ward, Marcus Crassus and the Late Roman Republic (Missouri 1977) is the most reliable account. Caesar's career is most authoritatively treated in M.Gelzer, Caesar, Politician and Statesman (Oxford 1968), and Zwi Yavetz, Julius Caesar and his Public Image (London 1983) is excellent on Caesar's legislation after 49 B.C. through which he aimed to become all things to all men. For Cicero, D.Stockton, Cicero, A Political Biography (Oxford 1971) is straightforward, while E.Rawson, Cicero (London 1975) gives a more rounded account. T.N.Mitchell, Cicero, The Ascending Years (Yale 1979) offers a most useful analysis of how a 'new man' could rise to the top. For a man who sought to create a rather different power-base in Rome, see A.W.Lintott, 'P. Clodius Pulcher - Felix Catilina', Greece and Rome 14 (1967) 157 ff. On the way in which the civil war of 49 B.C. split the Roman aristocracy, see D.R.Shackleton Bailey, 'The Roman Nobility in the Second Civil War', CQ n.s. 10 (1960) 253 ff.

For the groups in society outside the ruling aristocracy: C.Nicolet, L'Ordre équestre (Paris 1966) is fundamental on the equites but uses too narrow a definition (on which see T.P.Wiseman,

'The Definition of eques Romanus in the Late Republic and Early Empire', Historia 19 (1970) 67 ff). For the urban population of Rome see P.Brunt, 'The Roman Mob', Past and Present 35 (1966) 3ff.

The Politics of the Early Principate

Modern works on the politics of the early Principate are based on the ancient literary and documentary sources. Prime are the second century Annals of Tacitus, available in Loeb and Penguin translations (J.Jackson, 1956–70, and M.Grant, 1956, respectively), Suetonius' slightly later Lives of the Caesars (Loeb I and II by J.C.Rolfe, 1920; Penguin by R.Graves, 1957), and the History of Cassius Dio (Loeb V–VIII by E.Cary, 1917, 1955, 1924), which belongs a century after that. The evidence of papyri and inscriptions (particularly valuable for politicians' careers) has been gathered from comprehensive collections by V.Ehrenberg and A.H.M.Jones, Documents illustrating the Reigns of Augustus and Tiberius, second edn. by D.L.Stockton (Oxford, 1976) and E.M.Smallwood, Documents illustrating the Principates of Gaius Claudius and Nero (Cambridge 1967).

Amongst modern works, pride of place (not only for the English readers catered for here) must go to R.Syme's Roman Revolution (Oxford 1939), of which the last twelve chapters are devoted to the Principate of Augustus, and to his Tacitus (2 vols., Oxford 1958), especially section Vff. For the careers of individual senators, the Prosopographia Imperii Romani (first edn., Berlin 1897–8; second edn. (down to L), 1933–) is indispensable; S.J.de Laet, De Samenstelling van den romeinschen Senaat (Antwerp 1941), offers a list to be consulted with increasing caution as the years pass. E.Birley, 'Senators in the Emperor's Service', British Academy Proceedings 39 (1953) 197ff, has led readers to overestimate the attention paid by Principes to the talents of prospective senators; B.Campbell, 'Who were the "Viri Militares"?', JRS 65 (1975) 11ff. is sceptical of it even at the later stages; D.McAlindon, 'Entry to the Senate in the Early Empire' JRS 47 (1957) 191ff, is useful on the entry of men without senatorial antecedents; T.P.Wiseman's list in New Men in the Roman Senate extends to the reign of Augustus only. For the rules, see J.Morris, 'Leges annales under the Principate', Listy Filologicke 87 (1964) 316ff, and for the social background, see K.Hopkins, 'Elite Mobility in the Roman Empire', Past and Present 32 (1965) 12ff, reprinted in Studies in Ancient Society (ed. M.I.Finley, London 1974) 103ff. He refers to demographic factors, as also in Death and Renewal (Cambridge 1983) 31ff; this work also offers a realistic assessment of the political prospects of aristocrats and new men under the Empire (120ff). Figures (without regard for class) may be found in I.Kajanto, On the Problem of the Average Duration of Life in the Roman Empire (Helsinki 1968).

Many insights into the relations of the Senate and Princeps are to be found in R.P.Saller, Personal Patronage under the Empire (Cambridge 1982), and in A.H.M.Jones' collection of essays Studies in Roman Government and Law (Oxford 1960), especially in those entitled 'The Censorial Powers of Augustus', 'The Elections under Augustus', and 'Imperial and Senatorial Jurisdiction in the Early Principate' (the last two reprinted from JRS 45 (1955) 9ff, and Historia 3 (1955) 464ff, respectively). Of other writings on elections, the last chapter on E.S.Staveley, Greek and Roman Voting and Elections (London 1972), is not to be read without reference to different views, for example those of P.A.Brunt, 'The Lex Valeria Cornelia', JRS 51 (1961) 71ff, B.Levick, 'Imperial Control of Elections', Historia 16 (1967) 207ff, A.L.Astin, 'Nominatio in Accounts of Elections in the Early Principate', Latomus 28 (1969) 863ff, and A.J.Holladay, 'The Election of Magistrates in the Early Principate', Latomus 38 (1978) 874ff.

Political prosecution under the Principate has attracted much attention. The works of A.R.Bauman, The Crimen Maiestatis in the Roman Republic and Augustan Principate (Johannesburg 1967), and Impietas in Principem, a study of treason against the Roman Emperor with special reference to the first century AD (Munich 1974), are comprehensive, but suffer from a legalistic approach. R.S.Rogers, in Criminal Trials and Criminal Legislation under Tiberius (Middletown, Connecticut 1935), is preoccupied as usual with defence of the Princeps.

For the senatorial census, see most recently C.Nicolet, 'Le cens sénatorial sous la République et sous Auguste', JRS 66 (1976) 20ff. The view of money in senatorial life given by C. Rodewald's Money in the Age of Tiberius (Manchester 1976), chapter 1, on the financial crisis of A.D.33, must be modified: see the review E.Lo Cascio, JRS 68 (1978) 201ff. For the continual demands of status on senatorial purses, see D.Daube, 'The Protection of the Non-Tipper', in Roman Law: Linguistic, Social and Philosophical Aspects (Edinburgh 1969) 117ff.

J.Crook, Consilium Principis (Cambridge 1955), reveals the part played by the senatorial committee under Augustus and by its successors under later emperors, when it included men from outside the Senate. Prominent individuals such as Sejanus, Agrippina the Younger, Narcissus, and Pallas may also be studied in standard works devoted to the separate principates; the freedmen have been accorded special study: A.M.Duff, Freedmen in the Early Roman Empire (Oxford, 1928; repr. 1958); P.R.C.Weaver, Familia Caesaris, a Social Study of the Emperor's Freedmen and Slaves   (Cambridge 1972). For the role of the people, diminished as it was, Z.Yavetz, Plebs and Princeps (Oxford 1969), is excellent, and the ideology of the senatorial class has been well handled by Ch. Wirzubski in Libertas as Political Idea at Rome during the Late Republic and Early Principate (Cambridge 1960)

Addendum

Two important works on the Julio-Claudian period which appeared too late to be taken into account in this book are: Miriam T. Griffin, Nero: the End of a Dynasty (London 1984); and D.C. Braund, Augustus to Nero: a Sourcebook on Roman History, 31 B.C. – A.D. 68 (London 1984), which provides translations of documentary sources, including most of the items in Ehrenberg & Jones and Smallwood (p. 73 above).

Biographical Notes

Barbara Levick, Fellow and Tutor in Ancient History at St Hilda's
College, Oxford, since 1959, is the author of Roman Colonies in
Southern Asia Minor (1967), Tiberius the Politician (1976), and The
Government of the Roman Empire (forthcoming), and editor of The
Ancient Historian and his Materials (1975). She is currently
preparing an edition of monuments from Phrygia.

Jeremy Paterson is Senior Lecturer in Ancient History and Senior
Tutor in Arts at the University of Newcastle upon Tyne. His
research interests concentrate on Roman social and economic
history, particularly the Roman wine trade. He is working
currently on the writers on agriculture and writing a book on Roman
trade.

T.P.Wiseman is Professor of Classics at the University of Exeter.
His books include New Men in the Roman Senate (1971), Cinna the
Poet (1974), Clio's Cosmetics (1979) and Catullus and his World
(1985).

Index

Augustus   7f, 45f, 48

boni (see also optimates)   16

Caesar (see also 'first triumvirate')   7, 21f, 25

Catiline, conspiracy of   14, 15, 22, 36

Cicero, motivation of   10-12, 24

competition   12f, 29, 50, 52, 59

concordia ordinum   26f, 37

consilia   14-16, 48f

Crassus (see also 'first triumvirate')   7, 23

dangers of political life   23f, 56f, 63

dignity of Senate   48

domi nobiles (see also novi homines) 32f, 49f, 56

elections   28f, 33f, 50-2

envy   12

equites   29f, 62

factio   13f, 35f

'first triumvirate'   10, 14, 36

freedmen 27, 63

funeral orations 3f, 8, 13

law courts
(see also maiestas, prosecutions) 31,48

maiestas 56-8

military qualifications 32, 54f

nobilitas, definition of 50

novi homines
(see also domi nobiles) 30, 49f, 54, 56

opposition to principate 46, 62f

optimates (see also boni) 37

'opting out' 60-2

oratory 31f, 55

'parties' 35f

patrician privileges 61

patronage 31f, 34f, 38f

political issues 36f, 45f, 64

Pompey (see also 'first triumvirate') 7, 30f

popular assemblies 27f

popular demonstrations 59

populares 37f

principate, effect of
8-10, 39, 45f, 49, 52f, 54f, 56, 63f

prosecutions (see also law-courts) 55-7

publicani 29f, 35

Senate purges 47

senatorial committee 48

'Social War' 27

sponsione provocare   4

succession to principate   46f

Sulla, effect of   23-7

tabulae triumphales   4f

triumph   4, 22

triumphal decorations   8f

wealth   12f, 58-60